The Original Robin Hood

Traditional Ballads and Plays including all Medieval sources

translated by
Thor Ewing

WELKIN BOOKS

First Published 2020
Welkin Books Ltd

ISBN 978-1-910075-13-5

Acknowledgements

It isn't always possible to know who has influenced you on your journey towards making a book. Looking back, I can be fairly sure that Sean Breadin will have been one as, in the early 1990s, we performed and recorded several of the Robin Hood songs that have now found their way into this book; at this remove however, it's hard to pin down exactly how. No doubt other friends that I shared these songs with at the time have also influenced my thinking in one way or another.

More recently, as this book reached its final stages, I've made contact with some of the community of Robin Hood enthusiasts, scholars and researchers, and have found everyone very friendly and generous with their thoughts and ideas. Here I should mention in particular Rob Lynley, David Pilling, Henrik Thiil Nielsen and Stephen Basdeo. I'm indebted to Henrik Thiil Nielsen who, after I had already completed my initial translation of the *Gest*, took me through some important new points raised by his recent work on the text. Needless to say, responsibility for any errors is mine alone.

As ever, I must also mention my family, who have put up with my Robin Hood obsession with their usual forbearance.

And I should also thank you, the reader: I hope you enjoy this book.

TE

Contents

Preface

No one could be more surprised than me that this book should suggest there might have been a real Robin Hood. I had always been persuaded by the most sceptical of readings of the legend, and took it to be simply a legend and no more. Perhaps, it was this very focus on the legend itself that led me to a different conclusion about its history.

In trying to strip the legend back to its roots, I decided to follow only medieval sources and whatever traditional sources seemed to have escaped the influence of later literary re-imagination. As the oldest surviving sources, the medieval material is obviously of primary importance. Through studying legends and oral traditions, I have seen how traditional narratives can also be extremely conservative when it comes to preserving certain kinds of information. This led me to look more closely at the one traditional account of Robin Hood's birth, and to explore the possibility that the family relationships it suggests might actually reflect the oldest form of the story.

Somewhat to my surprise, this overlooked eighteenth-century source seemed to tally perfectly with medieval sources, including the earliest reference to Robin Hood in the fourteenth-century poem *Piers Plowman* and the dating for Robin Hood in three fifteenth-century chronicles. It also explained the curious fascination with Robin Hood in Scotland from at least the 1400s, and the equally curious trust and friendship between Robin and the sheriff's wife portrayed in a fifteenth-century ballad.

Until just a matter of weeks ago, I thought of Robin Hood simply as a generic name for any outlaw, and imagined that tales of any and every medieval highway ruffian had been combined to create the legend. As I write this, I am convinced that there is more to it than that, and that there may very well have been a real Robin Hood whose story is far more extraordinary than I had imagined. Many of the individual exploits set down in his legend may indeed have been added by later storytellers, but at the heart of Robin Hood's story is a life more extraordinary than any rumbustious adventure with longbows and quarter staffs. But then, it is only the most extraordinary real lives that give birth to legends.

TE

September 2020

Introduction

The modern image of Robin Hood starts with a nineteenth-century storybook which turned Robin into a hero fit for Victorian readers. The Robin we see on our screens today still carries the spirit of these wholesome Victorian adventure tales or 'ripping yarns'—but there was an earlier Robin Hood.

The earliest reference to 'rhymes of Robin Hood' is in the poem *Piers Plowman* written in 1377, and there are still medieval rhyming poems about Robin Hood which survive to this day. These old rhymes were an important part of the popular literature of the Middle Ages, despised by the cultured elite but loved by 'the common people'.

The English spoken 600 years ago is difficult for modern readers to understand, so the poems have been accessible only to the elite who cared so little for them in the past. Although many people might have known these old poems existed, they have usually had to rely on what other people say about them.

The aim of this book is to put the old poems, ballads and plays of Robin Hood back into a language that anyone can enjoy.

The oldest poems of Robin Hood

Some of the poems and ballad texts in this book survive in manuscripts and printed books from the 1400s. Some others are known today only from later copies, but were passed down from versions known in the fifteenth century. Some may have been heavily reworked from medieval originals in later centuries, and one or two were perhaps completely new creations based on old tradition. Although in this book the ballads are arranged in narrative order, they could also be grouped according to their age.

The first group is the texts which survive from the 1400s. These medieval texts include *A Gest of Robin Hood* which was probably composed in about 1450, and for which the oldest surviving copy was printed in about 1495. Aside from the *Gest*, there are only three other Robin Hood texts from before the year 1500: the earliest manuscript of 'Robin Hood and the Monk' is dated to shortly after c.1465; 'Robin Hood and the Potter' to c.1468; and the play of 'Robin Hood and the Sheriff' to c.1475. The dates for these written texts are somewhat tentative, but there does seem to be a curious cluster in the reign of King Edward IV. Because the audience for the Robin Hood ballads was not remotely bookish, the sparse medieval written record does not reflect the popularity of the songs in performance.

Next come the texts which were probably known in the Middle Ages, but which only survive in later copies. In this group are 'Robin Hood and Guy of Gisburn' and 'Robin Hood's Death' which both survive in the seventeenth-century Percy Folio but, whereas the text of 'Guy of Gisburn' is relatively complete and seems to closely reflect a lost medieval original, the text of 'Robin Hood's Death' in the same manuscript has literally been ripped to shreds, so the version in this book draws on other sources to make good the loss. 'The Play of Robin Hood' comes from an extended edition of the *Gest* which was printed in the mid-1500s; it was probably first performed as a play shortly before it first appeared in print.

Robin Hood ballads remained very popular in seventeenth-century England, and the new demand for printed ballad texts led to a boom in ballad production. There is a vast amount of this later Robin Hood balladry, but too many of these later works simply retell the story of Robin's encounter with yet another stranger in terms similar to his encounters with the Pinder or with the Curtal Friar. There is also a distinctive new jovial tone which transforms the spirit of the legend. Whereas the focus of the older ballads is on the narrative itself, the new style focusses on what the balladeer can make of it—rather than a story told in song, many of these later ballads are jolly songs based around a story.

In some cases however, a lost medieval ballad may have been a direct source for what is essentially a new text composed in the seventeenth or even eighteenth century. We can glimpse this process at work in the case of 'Robin Hood's Death' which survives in two very different texts, and the recent discovery of the Forresters Manuscript has shed similar light on other ballads.

Whenever there is no direct evidence for an early origin, it's often assumed that a ballad is a late creation but, if we rely too heavily and consistently on this approach, it could lead us into false assumptions about the overall spirit of the earlier legend. Although it might be hard to prove that any one of the later ballads definitely had a medieval origin, the Robin Hood tradition tended to rework old and well-known tales more often than creating entirely new ones. Because so little survives from the 1400s (and nothing at all from before 1450) it would be unwise to imagine that the surviving medieval sources alone can reveal the whole meaning of the medieval legend of Robin Hood.

Robert, Earl of Huntingdon

Ever since Bishop Thomas Percy pointed out in 1765 that 'the most ancient poems on Robin Hood make no mention of his earldom,' it has been accepted by cautious scholarship that no such earldom ever was. Modern scholars are all but unanimous in the belief that the

Robin Hood of medieval legend was a yeoman hero through and through, and that his connection with the Earls of Huntingdon did not exist before it was written into his story by the playwright Anthony Munday at the end of the sixteenth century. As there are no known references to the Earldom of Huntingdon in earlier texts, it might seem self-evident that the whole Earl of Huntingdon story was invented by Munday to gentrify this working-class hero for a new elite audience. But it is also possible that Munday had rediscovered the value of a genuine element of Robin Hood oral tradition which had merely been downplayed in fifteenth-century written texts.

This suggestion is strengthened by Richard Grafton's *Chronicle at Large* printed in 1568, which claims Robin Hood 'descended of a noble parentage, or rather being of a base stock and lineage, was for his manhood and chivalry advanced to the noble dignity of an Earl.' Although Grafton makes no mention of Huntingdon, his reference to Robin's noble blood predates Munday's plays by some thirty years. Curiously, Grafton introduces a note of uncertainty over Robin's pedigree, which he refers to as both 'noble' and 'base'.

In 1586, William Warner described Robin Hood as 'A County', meaning that he had the title of a count or earl named after a particular county. Warner doesn't specify the county in question, presumably because he regarded it as common knowledge. Warner's poem *Albion's England* introduces the Robin Hood theme enigmatically, slowly revealing Robin's identity through a succession of clues, of which his rank as 'A County' is the first. This literary conceit would have failed completely if there had been room for debate over whether Robin was or was not an earl, so Warner must have expected his readers to be completely familiar with the tradition associating Robin Hood with an earldom.

13

It is of course true that the earliest ballads do not mention Robin Hood's earldom, but the same is also true of later ballads composed when the tradition that Robin was Earl of Huntingdon was certainly well established. The notable exception is Matthew Parker's 120-verse *A True Tale of Robin Hood* of 1632 but, as a published work by a known writer, this is more a literary creation than a genuine example of popular balladry. In most ballads of Robin Hood, his claim to an earldom is simply irrelevant and would interfere with the narrative. Instead of the aristocratic 'Robert, Earl of Huntingdon', who might be a somewhat distant figure to the ordinary people who formed the main audience for these ballads, he is presented as plain 'Robin Hood', the everyman hero who is a friend to all honest men and women.

We naturally assume that the oldest surviving texts preserve the oldest features of the story, and that wherever newer texts differ from older ones it is because they have deliberately introduced a new feature to the legend—put simply, that they have made it up. But the Robin Hood poems, ballads and plays which survive from the fifteenth and sixteenth centuries clearly represent only a fraction of what could have been known to a fifteenth-century minstrel. And whereas today we rely solely on the surviving texts for our understanding of the original Robin Hood legend, medieval audiences may well have come to these ballads with a background knowledge based on other more informal forms of traditional lore.

The Earldom of Huntingdon happens to have been vacant at a crucial time in its history when Robin Hood might genuinely have claimed it, but it would have taken an unusual level of antiquarian interest for an Elizabethan playwright to establish this fact. That same interest in historical accuracy isn't seen elsewhere in the plays about Robin Hood and indeed, by mistakenly insisting on a historical setting in the reign of King Richard the Lionheart, they shift the action to an era before the earldom became vacant.

Randolf, Earl of Chester

The first known reference to Robin Hood is in the fourteenth-century poem *Piers Plowman*, in which the character of Sloth declares that, although he doesn't know the Lord's Prayer:

I know rhymes of Robin Hood and Randolf, Earl of Chester

It may be that Sloth is referring to two quite separate heroes, but a more natural reading would suggest that, for a fourteenth-century audience, the names of Robin and Randolf were somehow inextricably linked.

There were three Randolfs or Ranulfs who were medieval Earls of Chester: Ranulf le Meschin, 1070-1129; Ranulf de Gernon, 1099-1153; and Ranulf de Blondeville, 1170-1232. Following his theory that Randolf, Earl of Chester, is the hero of a similar but unrelated story to the legend of Robin Hood, the scholar James W. Alexander suggested that the Randolf in question is Ranulf de Gernon, who was Earl of Chester from 1128 until his death in 1153, and he presented Ranulf's career as equivalent to that of an outlaw. But Ranulf de Gernon seems never to have been celebrated in popular stories and, more recently, Glyn Burgess has refocussed attention on the better-known Ranulf de Blondeville who was the grandson of de Gernon, and who held the earldom from 1181 until 1232. Unlike his grandfather, this Randolf, Earl of Chester, was indeed a popular hero who was remembered in stories until at least the seventeenth century, but what is yet more remarkable about Ranulf de Blondeville is his close link with the Earldom of Huntingdon.

In 1190, Ranulf's sister Matilda married David of Scotland, Earl of Huntingdon (d.1153). This Earl of Huntingdon was a relative of William the Conqueror, descended from the mighty Anglo-Saxon earls of Northumbria, and he was the grandson of David I, King of

Scots. His elder brothers held the Scottish throne in turn as King Malcolm the Maiden and King William the Lion, and his descendants would include both King John Balliol and King Robert the Bruce.

Apart from the reference in *Piers Plowman* mentioned above, there is one other surviving reference to Robin Hood's connection with Randolf, Earl of Chester. This is in a recently-discovered seventeenth-century manuscript known as the Forresters Manuscript (BL Add. MS 71158). In his edition of the Forresters Manuscript, Stephen Knight dismisses the possibility that this reference reflects genuine tradition, thinking it 'highly improbable' that such a late manuscript could have 'preserved the memory of an otherwise unknown relationship between the two characters', and suggesting the name Randolf was deliberately added as 'a specific literary reference' to *Piers Plowman*. But although *Piers Plowman* was still occasionally read in seventeenth-century England, it had not been printed since 1561 and can hardly have been widely recognised. It is unlikely that its passing reference to Robin Hood would ever have seemed especially significant, and it is only from the perspective of a modern Robin Hood scholar that this one line stands out among more than 7,000 lines of poetry.

Another problem with Knight's argument is that the presence of Randolf is entirely unexplained in the ballad, which apparently relies on the reader or listener's prior knowledge that Robin is Randolf's protégé. It would have been impossible for anyone to have understood this reference unless Randolf's association with Robin Hood was already well known and understood. Since Ranulf de Blondeville was still remembered in seventeenth-century stories, it seems very probable that his association with Robin Hood was also remembered among the traditions surrounding him, and that ballad audiences would have understood his role in Robin's story without reference to *Piers Plowman*.

'Robin Hood's Birth'

The only traditional source to focus directly on Robin Hood's ancestry is the ballad 'Robin Hood's Birth', which claims he was the illegitimate grandson of an unnamed Earl of Huntingdon. This is slightly different to the more familiar version known from Anthony Munday's plays and later chapbook sources, where Robin is presented as Earl of Huntingdon in his own right, without any discussion of how he came by the title. It seems most unlikely that the more complicated story told in the ballad is based on Munday's version. Either, Munday has encountered a simplified version of the older tradition as told in song, or he has deliberately simplified it himself to suit his own ends.

This legendary genealogy, as the illegitimate son of an earl's daughter and a serving man, might also underlie Grafton's hesitancy over whether Robin Hood was of 'base' or 'noble' lineage. As the son of a serving man, Robin is indeed a yeoman by birth but, as the grandson of an earl, he also has a claim to a noble title. If Robin was the only son of David of Scotland's eldest daughter Margaret (who had no sons by her husband Alan, Lord of Galloway) then, when his uncle John, Earl of Huntingdon, died in 1237, Robin may well have considered himself the rightful heir.

Margaret's sister Ada of Huntingdon seems not to have claimed the title for her son Henry de Hastings so, officially the Earldom of Huntingdon lapsed and remained vacant for a hundred years. It is around such lost honours that legends gather, but a vacant earldom may also have attracted real claimants. Could it be that Ada of Huntingdon did not claim the Earldom of Huntingdon because her nephew Robin had a better claim than her son, but the king refused to acknowledge the right of a commoner's son to inherit a noble title?

As a traditional source recorded from oral testimony, and as the only original source for Robin Hood's ancestry, the ballad of 'Robin Hood's Birth' has a special place. Although the ballad is only recorded in later tradition, some late ballads seem to have had much earlier origins. In the case of this ballad however, there is an unusually strong body of opinion which claims that it cannot possibly be based upon ancient tradition.

There are three main arguments against an ancient origin for the ballad of 'Robin Hood's Birth': firstly—and most importantly for its critics—it suggests that Robin was descended from the Earls of Huntingdon, and if this noble connection is a late addition to the legend then the ballad must also be late; secondly, it is not recorded before it surfaces in eighteenth-century Scotland, and it is never recorded in English sources; lastly, the ballad is unlike others within the Robin Hood tradition.

The first argument is clearly circular. If the connection between Robin and the Earls of Huntingdon comes from genuine medieval tradition, then it cannot be used to dismiss the possibility of a medieval origin for the ballad or for the traditions that lie behind it.

The second argument may at first seem more persuasive. It is certainly true that this ballad has survived only in Scotland, and that it went unrecorded until the 1700s. Yet, if Robin Hood was believed to be closely related to the Scottish kings—actually linking the ancient House of Dunkeld with the later line of Robert the Bruce—then the story of his birth would have had a particular resonance in Scotland which it did not have in England.

Scottish interest in the Robin Hood ballads has always been something of a puzzle. Despite what seems to be their thoroughly English subject matter, a great number of the traditional ballads of Robin Hood have been recorded in Scotland. But if Robin was always thought to be Scottish by descent, then the puzzle is solved. Robin's connection with ancient and medieval Scottish kings would also explain why the only three early chroniclers to mention his name, Andrew Wyntoun, Walter Bower and John Mair, are all Scots (see Appendices A and B). If Robin was closely related to the Scottish kings, then it's easy to see why this English outlaw attracted the attention of the chroniclers of Scotland's official history, yet was never mentioned by English historians.

As early as the fifteenth century, the English ballad tradition seems to have been at pains to emphasise Robin's yeoman role, so we should not necessarily expect to find relics of a more aristocratic past in the English ballad tradition. Unlike the early written texts for English ballads, Scottish ballads went largely unrecorded before the eighteenth century, so this ballad (or the tradition behind it) was passed on solely by word of mouth until then.

The third argument misses the essential difference between the story of the hero's birth, and stories about his deeds. If the spirit of 'Robin Hood's Birth' has little in common with the ballads of Robin Hood's fights and robberies in the green wood, that's because its different subject demands a different treatment. Nonetheless, although the enchanted atmosphere of 'Robin Hood's Birth' comes straight out of medieval romance, there is some overlap between this ballad and the ballads of 'Leesome Brand' and 'Willie o' Douglas Dale', and some details may well have changed over the centuries.

Ballad scholar F. J. Child was aware of two complete versions of 'Robin Hood's Birth' and one fragment recorded separately from oral tradition. There is some disagreement between the different versions which suggests they have diverged over time, but the text from Peter Buchan's *Ballads of the North of Scotland* has also been 'improved' by a literary hand, probably during the 1700s. All three agree that Robin's mother was a noblewoman; the text from Anna Gordon (also known as Mrs Brown of Falkland) makes her an earl's daughter, and Buchan's version says she was the daughter of the Earl of Huntingdon. All three are also agreed that Robin's father was of lower social rank than his mother, but whereas Buchan's version suggests he was 'Sprung frae sma pedigree', Gordon says he was 'come o high degree', and the Kinloch Manuscript calls him 'a knight's ae son'.

If this ballad is indeed based on ancient tradition, it would not necessarily mean that David of Scotland really did have an illegitimate grandson called Robin Hood, but it would suggest that Robin Hood's legendary connection with the Earldom of Huntingdon goes back to a time before its supposed origin in the plays of Anthony Munday. If there ever was a real outlaw who gave rise to the Robin Hood legends, he may have liked to be thought of as a displaced nobleman whether he was or not, or perhaps later medieval storytellers embellished his legend with a noble ancestry. But however outlandish and improbable it may seem, the possibility that a genuine historical Robin Hood really was closely related to the Scottish kings cannot or should not be lightly dismissed.

The original Robin Hood

For decades, Robin Hood enthusiasts have trawled medieval records for references to people who might in some way be linked to the legendary outlaw. A huge variety of possible Robins has been put forward, but these competing theories almost always 'explain away' the legend, suggesting it originated in a far more mundane reality. What follows is different. If Robin Hood has any significance, it is as the hero of legend. If we start by dismissing the legend as fiction, we are no longer looking for the real Robin Hood.

This is a period when known historical figures are often poorly represented in contemporary records, so the legend itself is necessarily our primary source for Robin's career. Occasional details may or may not be confirmed by legal records but, since part of the point of Robin's story is that he successfully evaded the medieval legal system, he is generally unlikely to appear in its records. The most we can expect from such records where they do occur, is to add brief glimpses into the wider context of a specific incident.

The core outline of this legendary biography, derived from early ballads, fifteenth-century chronicles and the *Gest*, is this: Robin Hood must have been born before the death of Randolf, Earl of Chester; he had a violent run-in with the law as a teenager; he supported the rebellion of Simon de Montfort, and was dispossessed as a result; for years or even decades he led a band of outlaws based in Barnsdale, Yorkshire, sometimes also operating in Sherwood, Nottinghamshire; he had a running feud with the Sheriff of Nottingham, whom he eventually killed; he was responsible for significant robberies against the Bishop of Hereford and the monks of St Mary's Abbey, York; Robin Hood's outlaws lived according to courtly standards, and he performed the duties of a lord towards his retainers; he used his loot to support the poor; finally, he was treacherously killed at Kirklees Priory, when he was already ill. This is legend, not history, but if we are to look for a real Robin Hood, we should look not just for someone who happens to match some chance detail, but for someone whose life could have inspired a legend.

If we do take this next step, and allow ourselves to imagine that this legendary Robin Hood reflected a real Robin, we can now work out when he would have lived. If Ranulf de Blondeville who died in 1232 was indeed his benefactor, we might guess that Robin was born at some time before about 1217; if his mother was the child of Ranulf's sister Matilda who married David of Scotland in 1190, he is unlikely to have been born before 1205 at the earliest; and if Robin claimed the title of Earl of Huntingdon as the only son of Earl David's eldest daughter Margaret of Huntingdon, he will have been born before her marriage to Alan of Galloway in 1209. So, if we match the legend of his birth with the historical dates, Robin Hood is most likely to have been born some time between 1205 and 1217, probably shortly before 1209.

This understanding of the legend would suggest that Robin's entire adult life was spent under the reigns of Henry III and Edward I. Disappointing as this might be for modern readers who have grown up with a Robin Hood who stands with King Richard the Lionheart against 'Bad' King John, it fits with earlier accounts of Robin's career: writing in 1408, the chronicler Andrew Wyntoun mentions Robin Hood in his entry for the year 1283, placing him a decade after the death of Henry III; in the 1440s, Walter Bower wrote that Robin was at large in 1266, just after Henry III had defeated Simon de Montfort; and an anonymous fifteenth-century addition to Higden's *Polychronicon* also dates Robin Hood to the late thirteenth century (see Appendix A, 'Three fifteenth-century chronicles'). Furthermore, it is only in the late thirteenth century that the right characters are in place for the roles of Sheriff of Nottingham, Bishop of Hereford and Abbot of St Mary's, York.

The first writer to link Robin with the reigns of King Richard and King John was John Mair in 1521, who readily concedes that his dating is based merely on his own conjecture (see Appendix B, 'A sixteenth-century chronicle'). All earlier writers had believed that Robin had flourished in the second half of the thirteenth century, so there is no reason to suppose that the legend was ever associated with the era of Richard the Lionheart until more than three hundred years after King Richard's death.

THE GENEALOGY OF ROBIN HOOD

AS DERIVED FROM MEDIEVAL AND TRADITIONAL SOURCES

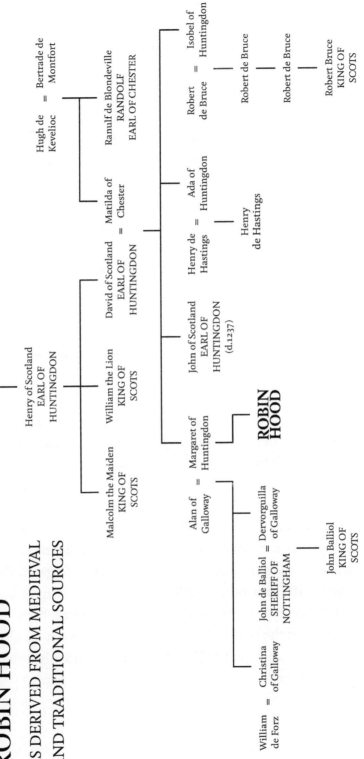

This original thirteenth-century dating casts Robin Hood in a very different life setting. Robin lived under a deeply unpopular king, who spent a year as the captive of a parliamentary government led by Simon de Montfort. It was an era of conflict over the limits of the royal hunting forest, when it was claimed that Sherwood was not legally royal forest at all. Disputes over forest boundaries would drag on until the reign of King Edward III, during which time the king's forest officers could still try to impose the old repressive forest law which had supposedly been replaced in 1217 by the new Charter of the Forest.

According to the ballad 'Robin Hood and the Foresters' (also called 'Robin Hood's Progress to Nottingham') when Robin was just 15 years old he killed fifteen foresters who had tried to cheat him out of twenty marks. Although this ballad is first recorded in the seventeenth century, it is quite unlike the later ballads. Its story is also told in the sixteenth-century Sloane Manuscript, and it is almost certainly based on medieval tradition. Details in the ballad are undoubtedly fictionalised and exaggerated, but if there is any grain of truth to this depiction of the young Robin as an *enfant terrible*, he would presumably have gone into hiding rather than face justice for such a crime. If the range of dates suggested above for Robin Hood's birth is correct, this incident should have occurred between c.1220–32.

As it happens, a Robin Hood appears as a fugitive from justice in the Pipe Rolls for the York Assizes of 1225, which value 'the goods of Robert Hood, runaway' (*catallis Roberti Hood fugitivi*) at 32 shillings and 6 pence. It is a perfect fit for the outlaw of legend. The next two entries list two other fugitives whose goods have been seized, including one William Warin—could this perhaps be William, brother of the outlaw Fulk Fitz Warin, whose story also involves Robin's protector, Randolf, Earl of Chester? And might there be some link between their crimes? This record says no more.

Robin's impetuous misdeed might have been motivated by more than a mere fit of pique at being cheated out of his winnings. In the winter of 1223-4 Robin's great uncle Randolf, Earl of Chester, was among the barons who tried to resist attempts by the regent Hubert de Burgh to take over the sheriffdoms and, as foresters, Robin's victims would have been acting as agents of Hubert de Burgh or his sheriffs.

Details from the ballad matched to the Pipe Roll fit the possible date range for Robin's birth, so these legendary details are consistent with history. If he was 15 when he met a party of foresters in 1223-4, then Robin was born in c.1208, a year before Margaret of Huntingdon's marriage to Alan of Galloway. This seems very plausible.

In further legal records, a 'Robert Hod' is listed among men who tear down dykes and hedges at Byland Abbey in the North Riding of Yorkshire in 1254, and the name occurs again among men who in 1262 had defaulted on a summons for robbing Saero de Gargrave at Ottringham in the East Riding. It may be significant that the town of Ottringham had been liable for goods seized from the William Warin named alongside Robert Hood in the Pipe Roll for 1225. Ottringham is in Holderness, where Little John (in the guise of 'Greenleaf') claims he was born in the *Gest*, and where, according to the Chronicle of Meaux, there were disturbances against the king in about 1260. However, as neither of these events is part of the known legend, even if they do relate to the same Robin, they are essentially incidental.

A medieval record from 1262 has also been viewed as a reference to Robin Hood, when a felon in Berkshire is described as 'William Robehod, runaway' (*Willelmi Robehod fugitivi*). It has been argued that William was given the nickname of 'Robehod' because he was a fugitive from justice, just as Robert Hood had been thirty years before. If so, then Robin Hood must already have developed a reputation as the definitive outlaw. This would suggest there was something remarkable about Robin's story, which was already attracting popular attention—perhaps, because he claimed the right to a vacant earldom? However this was before surnames were common, so most people used their father's name as a 'surname' and, since William's father's name is given in another document as 'Robert the smith' (*Robert le fevere*) we cannot be sure that William Robehod is named after the outlaw of legend.

According to the fifteenth-century chronicler Walter Bower, Robin Hood came to prominence in 1266, as a beacon of resistance after the defeat of the rebel barons at the Battle of Evesham. Just two years before, the barons led by Simon de Montfort had swept to power at the Battle of Lewes. They had held the recalcitrant king as their prisoner, and instituted a new system of government involving a council and an elected parliament. It may not have been much like the democracies of modern times, but it was a step towards greater political freedom. Although the powerful barons gained most, there were rights and freedoms for commoners too and inevitably, people looked to the reformers in hope of a better, fairer government for everyone in England. We will never know if this new government would ultimately have proved fairer than the rule of the king because in 1265, Simon de Montfort was defeated and killed at the Battle of Evesham by the young Prince Edward, eldest son of King Henry III.

The rebel leader Simon de Montfort was a relative of Robin's grandmother and of Randolf, Earl of Chester, so it is possible that Robin and Simon had known each other from Simon's first arrival in England in 1229. More certainly, one of Simon's most loyal supporters was Henry de Hastings who, as the son of Ada of Huntingdon, would have been Robin's cousin. Henry de Hastings fought for Simon de Montfort both at Lewes and at Evesham, and it was to his castle at

Kenilworth that the rebels retreated after their defeat at Evesham in 1265, where they were besieged by the king until mid-December. Another group of rebels held out on the Isle of Ely until the summer of 1267. Peace terms were offered in the Dictum of Kenilworth, but rebels who refused to come to terms were stripped of their legal right to lands and goods, and so effectively outlawed *en masse*.

According to an Assize Roll of 1269 from Cambridge, one Robert Hod had been among those on the island who chose not to accept the terms of the Dictum of Kenilworth, along with Robert's son Roger, Roger's servant Peter Giffard and a William Page who may have been Robin's page. This fully corroborates Walter Bower's account of Robin Hood's outlawry. Legal records alone cannot reveal the connection between a Robert Hood in a Yorkshire Pipe Roll for 1225 and another in a Cambridgeshire Assize Roll for 1267, but both records serve to confirm incidents in the oldest traditional accounts of Robin Hood's life, and so the legend itself is the connecting thread.

Could it be then that Robin Hood led a hundred or so disaffected rebels north from Ely into hiding in the forest just as Bower says? There is a theory that one Roger Godberd of Swannington did just that, and that the story of Robin Hood is based on this real-life, thirteenth-century thug. However, surviving records do not bear out every claim that has been made about the parallels between Godberd and Robin Hood. Certainly, Godberd fought for Simon de Montfort but, rather than continuing to resist royal authority, Godberd had in fact accepted the king's pardon for his part in the rebellion, so he was neither disinherited nor outlawed—indeed, as late as 1287 Godberd was recorded as owning lands in Leicestershire. Godberd had a history as a bully who used force to gain advantage over property rights, even taking his own parents to court on false charges. He claimed to have kept the peace after his royal pardon in December 1266, but was accused of crimes across a wide area of Leicestershire, Nottinghamshire and Wiltshire, including a robbery at Stanley Abbey in Wiltshire in 1270. Most of these crimes probably occurred well outside the areas traditionally associated with Robin Hood, and none is connected with Robin Hood's traditional haunt of Barnsdale in Yorkshire.

Incidents from Godberd's career could have influenced some episodes in the tales of Robin Hood but, although Roger Godberd was sometimes in Nottinghamshire at the time of Robin Hood, this does not make him Robin Hood. Godberd was perhaps the most notorious robber and murderer of his day, but the legend of Robin Hood was never that he robbed and killed more people than anyone else— instead Robin Hood stood for a different vision of society, one that is both 'courteous' and 'good'.

It would be naïve to imagine that robbing and killing weren't integral to Robin Hood's career, but they are not enough to form the basis of the popular legend. Instead, the legend presents Robin Hood as holding court in the green wood just as a king or earl would hold court in their palaces. The court of Robin Hood challenges the hierarchy of king and sheriff in its very existence as an alternative realm beyond the bounds of ordinary society. It proclaims that, just as the king has rejected the new vision of society heralded by Simon de Montfort, so now Simon's followers have rejected the laws and customs of the king and have founded a colony under their own rule.

While Walter Bower sets Robin in the year 1266, the slightly earlier chronicler Andrew Wyntoun mentions Robin Hood in his entry for 1283 during the reign of King Edward I. This was the year of the momentous Parliament of Acton Burnell, the first time an English king ever allowed commoners to take a role in government, the very cause that Simon de Montfort had fought and died for twenty years earlier. If Robin Hood was indeed born in 1208 he would have been 75 years old in 1283 which may seem unexpectedly elderly, but the *Gest* says he lived in the green wood for 'twenty years and two' which, if reckoned from 1266, would take us to 1288, while the Sloane Manuscript claims he lived to the ripe old age of 87. Wyntoun's account is unusual in associating Robin with Inglewood in Cumberland, far to the north of anywhere mentioned elsewhere in his legend, and he may have been only vaguely familiar with the details of Robin Hood's story. But despite potential difficulties, it is appealing to imagine that Robin is reconciled with the king only when Simon de Montfort's political reforms are finally enacted.

An even later date is assigned to Robin Hood by the one reference linked with an English chronicle, which was discovered recently by Julian Luxford. *Polychronicon* was an important and popular history by the fourteenth-century chronicler Ranulf Higden, which survives in more than a hundred manuscripts. Whilst Higden himself does not actually mention Robin Hood in *Polychronicon*, this omission was made good in one manuscript by a late fifteenth-century scribe who added a brief note under the section on the 1290s to say that, around this time Robin Hood had lived as an outlaw in Sherwood. This dating is only very slightly later than the date of 1288 suggested by reading the *Gest* in the context of the Battle of Evesham. Although such a long career may stretch the limits of historical plausibility for a real-life outlaw, these accounts are not direct records of historical fact so much as early versions of the legend and as such, may be based on exaggerated claims. Overall, it is striking that the three earliest chronicle references all independently date Robin Hood to the second half of the thirteenth century. Fifteenth-century writers seem to have universally accepted the reality of Robin Hood as a particular historical person, and they all agreed on roughly when he had lived.

The Sheriff of Nottingham

Robin Hood is famous for his feud with the Sheriff of Nottingham. It is the way of legends to emphasise the personal and the dramatic but in reality, if Robin lived as an outlaw for any length of time, he would have contended with several sheriffs. It was the sheriff's job to uphold the king's law and justice, and the Sheriff of Nottingham had a special duty to maintain the royal forests, so Robin Hood's struggle with the sheriff may have been inevitable. It is curious however that an outlaw based largely in Yorkshire should not have found his chief opponent in his local sheriff, the Sheriff of York.

Unsurprisingly, the role of sheriff was open to abuse. Robert Vavasour held the post of Sheriff of Nottingham from 1236 to 1239, and again from 1246 until May 1255, when he was fined 200 marks and relieved of his responsibilities because he and his cronies had 'misconducted themselves to the king's great loss' and had done 'grievous injuries' to the Prior of Lenton. Vavasour was succeeded as sheriff by Roger Lovetot, who may have been no more trustworthy than his predecessor. Roger Lovetot's brother was Sir John de Lovetot, whose career as Justice of Common Pleas ended in disgrace with his imprisonment in the Tower and a hefty fine of 3,000 marks—enough to pay the wages of a hundred skilled labourers for a year.

Medieval sheriffs collected taxes from their counties for the king, and also collected extra revenue which they kept for themselves. According to the contemporary chronicler Matthew Paris, the sheriffs 'rode about with large retinues and oppressed all the country people by their exactions':

> '...the sheriffs and royal agents, without fear of being charged with offences, made it their whole business, on some fictitious

grounds or other, to impoverish, or rather to plunder, all they could ... They seized from the poor, and especially from traders, their horses, carts, wines, provisions, cloths, wax, and other necessaries, and even compelled the despoiled parties against their will to convey the goods seized to distant places ...'

Every sheriff was a fox in charge of a hen house. As the king's officer, the sheriff kept the king's law and the king's peace but, while on the one hand a medieval king was the embodiment of law and order, he might also be compared to a gangland boss, with his taxes serving as protection money. Offices such as Sheriff of Nottingham were awarded to the king's trusted henchmen. This was about straightforward personal loyalty to the man at the top, and there was little notion of public service for the common good. The sheriff defended the rights of the king against the people, and Robert Vavasour had incurred the king's wrath because he had acted against the king's personal interests.

Medieval government was based largely on bonds of trust. A strong and good king could inspire his followers, and control the excesses of his representatives—Henry III was not that king. Reforms were introduced by the council of barons who took control of government in 1258, but were largely undone again by the king in 1261.

The next sheriff was Simon de Headon, who was Sheriff of Nottingham from 1258 on-and-off until 1267. Simon de Headon sometimes shared his role as sheriff with one John de Balliol, and sometimes fulfilled the role on Balliol's behalf. While Simon de Headon was a prominent local landowner, John de Balliol was a player on an international stage with interests across England, France and Scotland. Chronicler Matthew Paris describes John de Balliol as a man of 'great power and influence' and as 'a rich and powerful knight':

'This same John was avaricious, rapacious and tenacious, far beyond what became him, and what was beneficial to his soul; and he had for a long time unjustly harassed and much injured the church of Tynemouth as well as that of Durham. He had also on divers specious pretexts worried and injured other churches, as well as knights and ecclesiastics, his neighbours...'

When King Henry III was at Nottingham in 1255, John de Balliol was accused of 'having acted unjustly and unfaithfully towards the kingdom of Scotland'. The king set off to discover the truth, but Balliol 'craftily made peace with the king, by supplying him in his necessity with money, of which he possessed abundance.' John de Balliol was also firmly opposed to the political reforms of Simon de Montfort, and fought for the king at the Battle of Lewes where he was forced to surrender but was allowed home on condition he would stand trial before parliament. Instead Balliol waged war against Simon de Montfort's supporters, capturing the Earl of Derby in May 1265.

As Sheriff of Nottingham, the 'rapacious' John de Balliol, enemy of Simon de Montfort, makes a particularly fitting opponent for Robin Hood. What is more remarkable is that, if Robin Hood was the illegitimate son of Margaret of Huntingdon as suggested by ballad tradition, it would mean that John de Balliol was married to Robin Hood's sister. Furthermore, through his wife Dervorguilla of Galloway, Balliol inherited much of the Honour of Huntingdon, the very lordship which Robin Hood claimed as his own. This means the rivalry between Robin and the Sheriff runs deeper than the inevitable struggle between law and outlaw—it is a family squabble. It is no doubt because of this personal relationship that Robin's great feud is with the Sheriff of Nottingham rather than the Sheriff of York, even though early sources link Robin Hood more closely with Barnsdale in Yorkshire than with Sherwood in Nottinghamshire.

This close family connection between sheriff and outlaw is also recalled in the ballad of 'Robin Hood and the Potter' where Robin is lavish in his gifts to the sheriff's wife, and expresses his love for her without any suggestion of impropriety. Robin Hood gives the sheriff's wife five pots, a gold ring and a white palfrey, and praises her virtue. For her part, the sheriff's wife invites Robin to dine at the sheriff's high table, laughs that Robin has outwitted her husband, and finally makes clear that she knew who he was all along. All this has puzzled previous editors, but makes perfect sense if we are expected to already know that the sheriff's wife was in fact Robin Hood's sister. It would be rash to imagine that the story of 'Robin Hood and the Potter' is literally true, but its fiction will have been woven from strands of pre-existing traditional lore, and the close relationship between Robin and the sheriff's wife appears to have been part of that lore.

According to both the *Gest of Robin Hood* and the ballad 'Robin Hood and Guy of Gisburn', the sheriff's feud with Robin Hood culminates in the sheriff's death. The death of the Sheriff of Nottingham may not always be a feature of modern retellings, but it seems to have been an essential part of the medieval legend. The chronicler Walter Bower refers to Robin Hood in Latin as *famosissimus sicarius*, which has been translated as 'a well-known cut-throat' and as 'most famous armed robber', but the word *sicarius* usually signifies an assassin or hitman, and Bower may have had a specific famous assassination in mind, perhaps the killing of the Sheriff of Nottingham. However, the credibility of the tradition that Robin killed the Sheriff of Nottingham is somewhat undermined by the disagreement between texts on how the sheriff came to be killed. According to 'Robin Hood and Guy of Gisburn' he was shot by Little John in Barnsdale (perhaps a mistake for Sherwood) while according to the *Gest* he was beheaded by Robin Hood on the streets of Nottingham.

John de Balliol died in 1268. Exactly where or how remains a mystery, but an oblation was made in Nottingham in John de Balliol's name at the time of his death, which it has been suggested was paid by his wife Dervorguilla. It is tantalising evidence that Balliol may have died in Nottingham or nearby. One year before Balliol's death, Simon de Headon, who sometimes undertook the position of Sheriff of Nottingham on Balliol's behalf, was suddenly succeeded in mid-term as sheriff by his son Gerard. Could it be that the death of the sheriff as told in the ballad of 'Guy of Gisburn' and the death as told in the *Gest* are both actually true, and that both these sheriffs met their end at the hands of Robin Hood and his men? If so, that would indeed justify his reputation as *famosissimus sicarius*.

The Bishop of Hereford

It seems odd at first that the Bishop of Hereford should be singled out for special attention in the ballads of Robin Hood. Why not the Archbishop of York, whose diocese covered both Sherwood and Barnsdale? Even the bishops of the neighbouring dioceses of Lincoln or Coventry would seem to make more sense. But there is in fact a good reason why it is the Bishop of Hereford who is specified.

Peter de Aigueblanche was Bishop of Hereford from 1240 until his death in 1268. He is viewed by historians as one of Henry III's most important administrators, and conducted international politics on behalf of the king including treaties with Castile and Savoy, but is mostly remembered for his fraudulent scheme to ensnare the English clergy in papal debt for the profit of the king. The chronicler Matthew Paris writes that Peter of Aigueblanche was 'notorious, for being most hostile and unfaithful to the kingdom ... indeed he was by force thrust into the bishopric of Hereford, and by the secular power [*i.e.* the king], and after fattening himself on the milk, wool and richness of the flock intrusted to him, he abandoned that flock ... to the fangs of wolves.'

Matthew Paris goes on to devote considerable attention to 'the evil counsel given by the bishop of Hereford', writing:

> 'About this same time Peter [Aigueblanche], bishop of Hereford (whose memory exhales a most foul and infernal odour), went to the king, whom he knew to be in need of money and to be striving to acquire it with his utmost endeavours, and whispered in his ear the following poisonous counsel: "My lord," said he ... "I will ... induce the pope to compel each and all of the prelates of England, even by force and against their will, to pay a large sum of money, so as fully to satisfy your wants." To this plan the king gave a hearty consent, and the two were highly pleased.'

With 'foxlike cunning' the bishop made the English churches liable for substantial debts to foreign merchants, such that 'if all previous oppressions were reckoned up together, they would be considered light in comparison with this infliction.' In this way, the Bishop of Hereford 'by his treachery injured the whole kingdom of England'.

Peter de Aigueblanche was a natural enemy for the supporters of Simon de Montfort, who commandeered his lands and possessions in 1263, and briefly imprisoned him in Eardisley Castle. It is hard to think of a more fitting person for Robin Hood to waylay than this target of popular hatred who was responsible for fraudulently raising money for the king, and his name has long been linked with the legend. The Dean of Hereford, James Wentworth Leigh, referred to this tradition in an article of 1901, writing, 'It is said, with what truth I know not, that he was the bishop who was stopped and robbed in Sherwood Forest by the famous Robin Hood.'

An earl and yet a yeoman

Robin Hood as grandson of David of Scotland is hardly the ancestry we would expect for a true English yeoman. But although this high-born Robin Hood might seem less appealing as a figurehead for class warriors, he is much more typical for a medieval hero. In medieval stories and legends, it is unusual to find any leading figure without a significant aristocratic or royal connection. There is often an underlying assumption that nobility is inborn, and that a noble character corresponds to a noble pedigree. Robin's inner nobility might be witnessed in his natural 'courtesy' and his munificence towards the knight in the *Gest*, while the loyalty shown by Robin's followers reveals him as a natural leader.

Robin Hood's kinship with kings also explains the respect shown to him by the King of England in the *Gest*, where the two leaders treat each other as equals. If Robin was the grandson of David of Scotland, then his close relative Alexander II, King of Scots, was married to the English king's sister, and King Alexander's son was married to the English king's daughter. Through his great grandmother Bertrade de Montfort, Robin was also related to Simon de Montfort, who was married to King Henry's sister, Eleanor of England.

The Robin Hood who emerges from this analysis is something of a surprise. He is at once a true commoner and a true lord. From his unique perspective, without a place in the medieval hierarchy, this Robin could have cast a critical eye on the structure of society, and may well have been especially alert to social justice and injustice.

It's even possible that Robin's surname holds a clue to his peculiar status outside the usual categories, and perhaps to his own attitude to his position. One meaning of the Middle English word 'hod' or 'hode' is 'rank' or 'status' so Robin Hood could mean something like 'Robin of Rank'—a fitting name for the man who was born without 'hod' so had to make his own. Such a man, leading a life in the green wood that was both physically and metaphorically outside society whilst claiming the status of an earl with a band of loyal, liveried retainers, may well have left little trace on the historical record, yet would inevitably inspire storytellers to embroider his legend.

Most scholars choose to emphasise Robin Hood's yeoman status, suggesting that if he is described in the earliest surviving poems as a yeoman then he cannot have been an earl, but it is far from clear that the concept of 'yeoman' had any real significance at the time when Robin is supposed to have lived. England in the fifteenth century had a large yeoman class. These yeomen or peasants were not the poorest of the poor, but were independent smallholders and artisans who made a living through their labour. But before the mid-fourteenth century, the old feudal social hierarchy had been more powerful; it was only after the devastation wrought by the Black Death that a new social order emerged, so it was only in later medieval England that the yeoman played an important part.

The earliest surviving Robin Hood narratives date from the fifteenth century and, although it is easy to assume they preserve the legend in its truest form, if earlier centuries had no clear concept of the rank of yeoman then, inevitably, the characterisation of Robin Hood as a yeoman must be a late-medieval addition to the legend. So, the principle argument against Robin Hood's aristocratic credentials (or pretensions) turns out to be built on sand.

Some scholars point out that the Robin Hood ballads preserve nothing of the political situation of the mid-thirteenth century—there is no mention for instance of Simon de Montfort, or the relative advantages of rule by king or council—but it would be a mistake to look to balladry to preserve the nuances of historical politics. The Robin Hood ballads concentrate on the deeds of their hero as an individual, and like all ballad literature they tend towards archetypal patterns and away from specific historical settings. Like medieval art, which portrays Biblical and Classical scenes in contemporary medieval dress, the medieval ballads portray their heroes in a non-historicised setting for more universal appeal. To treat ballads as if they were historical chronicles, expecting them to approach the past in the same terms, is to miss the distinction drawn between history and poetry by Aristotle, who wrote that whereas history as told in chronicles 'speaks of what has happened, [poetry speaks] of what can happen. So, poetry is more philosophical and significant than history, because poetry is really about universals, history about particulars.' It is as poetry and story that history becomes legend, distilling human meaning out of mere events.

This makes it all the more remarkable that key details of Robin Hood's legend, whether true or not, are so historically plausible. Despite the fact that the balladeers show no interest in matching their tale with the work of the chroniclers, the dates fit and there are other unexpected correspondences. Simply by following the traditional biography of Robin Hood, elements of the legend come sharply into focus—in particular Robin's relationship with Randolf, Earl of Chester, and his friendship with the sheriff's wife. And this Robin Hood would naturally be remembered better by Scottish chroniclers than by English ones, because he is said to be part of the family that links the ancient royal House of Dunkeld with the later kings of Balliol and Bruce; John de Balliol and Dervorguilla of Galloway were the parents of another John Balliol, who would reign as King of Scots from 1292 until 1296, while Robin's aunt Isobel married Robert de Bruce, 4th Lord of Annandale, whose son Robert would compete against John Balliol for the Scottish crown, and whose great grandson

Robert Bruce would be crowned King of Scots in 1306. From the viewpoint of a fifteenth-century Scottish chronicler, Robin's feud with John de Balliol, Sheriff of Nottingham, perhaps prefigures the feud between Bruces and Balliols in fourteenth-century Scotland.

The plausibility of the legend does not necessarily make it historically true, but does suggest that when the legend was first told, it was important for the details of the hero's life to fit the real historical facts. This takes us back more-or-less to the lifetime of the supposed Robin Hood, when the specific details were still so well remembered that they could shape the legend. In view of this, it no longer seems possible to argue that the name is simply a generic term for any outlaw, or that Robin Hood is an idealised representation of all forest outlaws (although inevitably, later outlaws styled themselves after the legendary Robin Hood). Instead, it seems entirely possible that there was once a real outlaw who claimed to be heir to the Earldom of Huntingdon after the death of John, Earl of Huntingdon, in 1237. In the strictly hierarchical world of the Middle Ages, such a claim may well have given him a natural position of power and authority, while it may simultaneously have seemed impossible for the son of a commoner to inherit a noble title. Whether or not there was any truth in this outlaw's boast, it was probably this claim to nobility more than anything else that paradoxically ensured his survival in legend as a yeoman hero.

Taking from the rich, giving to the poor

The chronicler John Mair wrote in 1521 that Robin Hood 'would allow no woman to be molested, nor would he steal the belongings of the poor, indeed he provided for them sumptuously on rich pickings from the abbots.' As Mair's account is largely if not solely informed by ballad stories, we may probably assume this theme is drawn from early ballads, but is there any trace of it in medieval and traditional sources?

Though there are few specific examples, Robin is consistently characterised as 'good' and, according to the *Gest* IV v.6 and VIII v.39, this includes benevolence to the poor. There is a firm rule in the *Gest* against robbing or harming ordinary working people (I, v.12-15) and, in ballads such as 'Robin Hood and the three Squires' or even 'Robin Hood and the Bishop of Hereford', Robin commits rightful crimes against wrongful authority.

Everyday poor relief rarely makes for a gripping story suitable for a ballad, but there is an exception in the ballad of 'Robin Hood and the Old Woman'. This ballad hinges on the fact that Robin Hood has previously given the old woman twelve pence to buy stockings and shoes. The old woman remembers Robin's kindness, and repays him by saving him from the sheriff in entertaining style. It may be only one ballad but, if Robin Hood has given money to this one old woman, how many other unnamed people might he have helped?

It is unlikely that a historical Robin Hood operated a coherent system to fairly and effectively redistribute the wealth of the rich among the poor, but his legend embodied the possibility of a fairer society where wealth inequalities were eased, and money could be used to help whoever needed it most.

Helping the very poorest is one thing, but why does the outlaw spend his time and effort helping a knight, one of the bastions of the established social hierarchy, to get back his lands, which are no doubt made profitable through the toil of working men and women? In the opening of the *Gest* (I, v.14) Robin Hood makes clear his view that knights are potential friends rather than natural enemies—as warrior leaders, good knights were essential to the order of a society that had no police. His support for this particular knight is vindicated when

Sir Richard goes out of his way to help a yeoman who has been wronged by a crowd of other yeomen at a wrestling match. The proper role of the knight is illustrated in the help he gives to a man of lower social rank. For Robin Hood or for the poet of the *Gest*, it is the role of the good knight to ensure fairness and order in society.

When the knight intervenes on the yeoman's behalf, the yeoman's antagonists are his social equals not his superiors. The separation between right and wrong in the *Gest* is not based on social rank. This is no class warfare. A good knight or a good king can use power for the good of the people, just as a bad sheriff can abuse his power. Since some form of social hierarchy is inevitable, it is the fundamental duty of those entrusted with power to use it for the benefit of the powerless.

Robin Hood takes the side of the knight against the monks of St Mary's Abbey, because the monks are driven solely by profit, whereas a good knight functions as the head of a community and has the welfare of his people at heart, just as Robin himself leads his merry men—he does not exploit lands and followers for profit, but works for the common good of the group and of society at large.

The Abbey of St Mary's, York, was the wealthiest monastic house in northern England, notorious both for its aggressive policy towards land rights and for the luxurious lifestyle of its abbots. In 1262, tensions between St Mary's Abbey and the town of York erupted into violence, in which the abbot's men were attacked and his property destroyed, as a result of which Abbot Simon de Warwick fled the city for two years. Simon de Warwick remained as abbot until his death in 1296, overseeing grandiose building projects. He is undoubtedly the abbot in the *Gest* and, as with the identification of the Sheriff of Nottingham and the Bishop of Hereford, this confirms a late thirteenth-century dating for the legend. The depiction of the monks of St Mary's Abbey eagerly anticipating their enjoyment of the knight's lands is carefully developed in the *Gest*, and the inference is that any enterprise devoted to accumulating excessive wealth is fundamentally opposed to human happiness and fulfilment—if money is the primary objective, people will be valued only inasmuch as they contribute to profit.

In the world of Robin Hood, money is there to be spent, shared and enjoyed in company with others. Generosity is the key. Whereas the monks hoard their wealth behind the walls of their monastery, Robin gives his wealth away to whoever needs it. In medieval thinking, it is the circulation of money which benefits society, whereas storing up unnecessary wealth has a negative impact. So, Robin encourages the knight to lead a more lavish lifestyle befitting his rank.

The later Middle Ages saw increasing frustration among churchmen that ordinary people cared more about Robin Hood than religion (see Appendix D, 'Some early allusions to the legend'). It's not just that they were seduced by escapist adventure stories, but these stories raised the prospect of a fairer society in this life, whereas the medieval Church preached that the only true justice lay beyond the grave. In an England where abbots lived in luxury, and bishops were in cahoots with kings to defraud the nation for personal gain, it's hardly surprising if the Christian message of heavenly rewards for earthly suffering may sometimes have met with a sceptical reception.

'Good Yeomanry'

For many modern readers, the violence in these old tales of Robin Hood comes as a shock, making the hero a much darker character than the Robin Hood of childhood imagination—almost an anti-hero. This reading has inspired some interesting interpretations of the old stories, but it's not how the original audience was expected to react.

Instead, the outlaws and their world are continually described as 'merry' and 'good', and often behave with a carefree good naturedness.

So, why might early audiences have forgiven Robin for his crimes? Perhaps, the medieval audience was simply more realistic about what life as an outlaw entailed. Perhaps, it was that they were all too familiar with violence and injustice sanctioned by 'lawful' authority, and were happy to imagine a world where the underdog for once had the upper hand. Both these suggestions may be true, but the legend of Robin Hood goes beyond general sympathy for tit-for-tat violence of the oppressed against their oppressors. As well as giving vent to a rebellious instinct against the misdeeds of the established elite, these stories encapsulate the rules of an alternative code of life for the ordinary yeomen, the independent peasant farmers, tradesmen and artisans of medieval England.

We are familiar with the medieval code of Chivalry which was supposed to guide the lives of the knights or 'chivalers' (from Old French, *chevaliers*). The ideals of Chivalry can be found in secular poetry written for the knightly and noble classes of society. This 'chivalric literature' includes the Arthurian romances and the *chansons de geste*. Robin Hood literature might not have such a prestigious pedigree, but if the *chansons de geste* embody the code of the knights, so the *Gest of Robin Hood* and the fifteenth-century Robin Hood ballads embody the code of the English yeoman.

Part of this code is made explicit near the start of the *Gest* (I, v.12–15) and it might almost be a deliberate inversion of elite values. The humble working people are to be left unharmed, but the great lords of the land and the princes of the church are fair game. Knights and squires, who formed a middle rank in medieval society, are seen as potential allies to be spared if they 'would be a good friend' (I, v.14, 'wol be a gode felawe').

The code as expounded in the *Gest* may never have been literally embraced by its audience. Most yeoman listeners probably had no intention to really 'beat and bind' their local bishop or archbishop as Robin recommends, but they may still have wholeheartedly upheld the spirit of his remarks. It's difficult or impossible to imagine the same sentiment from a bishop or archbishop, or indeed from anyone whose living was dependent on the patronage of those ranked above them in the feudal hierarchy. But by including knights and squires, the lowest rung of the gentry, within the yeoman's world, the *Gest* describes an apparently viable social order, with room for everyone except the great lords and princes of the church who took the greatest wealth from society to hoard for themselves.

It is in 'Robin Hood and the Potter' that we learn the name of this code of conduct. When the Potter berates Robin for trying to force payment out of a poor yeoman artisan instead of a rich lord or bishop, Robin quickly agrees and admits his fault with the words, 'You speak good Yeomanry' ('Thow seys god yeme[n]rey', I v.23). Robin also invokes the spirit of 'good Yeomanry' in the ballad 'Robin Hood and the Friar' when he urges the Curtal Friar to call off his dogs and 'keep good Yeomanry' (Percy Folio, 'save good yeomanry').

So, just as medieval knights or 'chivalers' lived by 'Chivalry', the medieval yeoman was encouraged to live by 'Yeomanry'. Like the word 'chivalry', which in Middle English also denoted a body of armed knights, the word 'yeomanry' could be used to refer to yeomen as a group. Also like Chivalry, or indeed like good neighbourliness, the code of Yeomanry is ill defined and may generally be seen as little more than a tacit understanding between men of a similar social class, but part of the role of ballads like these is to explore what it is that makes for good Yeomanry.

Even in the tales of Robin Hood however, not everyone lives up to the ideal of good Yeomanry. The knight in the *Gest* encounters a crowd of yeomen at Wentbridge who would rather kill a fellow competitor than award him the prize he has fairly won, and it is left to a knight to show the true spirit of Yeomanry and ensure fair play (*Gest*, II v.57–61). Even Robin himself fails to abide by the code of Yeomanry in 'Robin Hood and the Potter' as we have seen.

Just as knights did battle according to the rules of Chivalry, so yeomen were also apparently expected to face each other in a fair fight. Steadfastness in the face of violence is highly valued, but these fights end swiftly when one party admits defeat. The ability to endure violence seems more important than victory, and literary fights between yeomen are more likely to end in friendship than in death. Such violence can be highly formalised, as in the buffets given as forfeits in the *Gest* (VII and VIII). When Robin asks the king to take part, he tests him in the yeoman's world and finds that a king can make a good yeoman. When the king in turn asks Robin to share his world, Robin finds that, for all his courtesy, he cannot make a good courtier, yet the lesson is not that Robin is inferior to the court, but that court life is inferior to the life of a yeoman.

This concept of Yeomanry makes good sense in the fifteenth-century context which gave rise to the texts of the *Gest* and 'Robin Hood and the Potter', but does not so readily translate to the setting of earlier medieval England. Before the Black Death, there simply was no significant yeoman class of the kind envisaged by the Robin Hood texts which survive from the 1400s. Indeed, the modern sense of the word 'yeoman' as a freeborn commoner is essentially a late medieval development. So, it would seem that a pre-existing medieval legend was repurposed for the changed social context of later medieval England.

Attitudes to women

Unlike the nobleman's code of Chivalry which perhaps reaches its
height of expression in the Arthurian romances, there is no room for
Courtly Love in the more rugged code of Yeomanry. There was a tension
in chivalric literature between love on the one hand and marriage on
the other, and this is an area which Robin Hood literature studiously
avoids. There are no women in the green wood of the ballads and the
Gest, where the bond of brotherly camaraderie between the outlaws is
enough. Yeomanry as expressed in the Gest and ballads is very much
a code for men's behaviour, but it teaches respect towards women
through Robin's own courtesy and his faith in the Virgin Mary:

> Robin so loved Our dear Lady
> > That, for fear of deadly sin,
> He would never harm the company
> > That any woman was in.
>
> > > (Gest, I v.10)
>
> For the love of Our Lady,
> > All women he did revere.
>
> > > (Robin Hood and the Potter, I v.3)
>
> I never hurt woman in all my life,
> > Nor at my end shall it be.
>
> > > (Robin Hood's Death, v.44)

Just as the knights of romance rescue their damsels in distress, so
Robin is devoted to the protection of women, but the difference of
emphasis is significant. Whereas the women in chivalric literature
are typically young and beautiful maidens, Robin is more likely to
encounter mothers and older women. In the Gest, the knight's wife

appeals to Robin to rescue her husband, and in 'Robin Hood and the three Squires' a woman of Nottingham appeals to him to rescue her sons; in 'Robin Hood and the Potter' Robin showers his sister the sheriff's wife with gifts, while in 'Robin Hood's Death' he meets first with an old woman kneeling on a plank over the river, and then with his cousin the Prioress of Kirklees.

The one ballad where a woman does take a prominent role is the aptly named 'Robin Hood and the Old Woman' (although the Forresters Manuscript calls her an 'old wife', the word 'wife' did not originally mean 'spouse'). For this story, an old woman is perhaps chosen because she represents the most marginalised group in ordinary, settled medieval society. But although Will Scarlock voices a stereotypically negative view of old women, describing her as a 'witch', the shallowness of his judgement is revealed when it turns out he has really seen Robin Hood disguised in the old woman's clothes.

The ballad actually shows the old woman in a very positive light. She is witty and resourceful, and relishes the chance to redeem what she sees as her debt to Robin Hood for his charity towards her. She is portrayed as a thoroughly independent character, who takes full command of the narrative to restore Robin to a position of power and safety, for which he rewards her with a substantial gift.

For all that women generally play little part in the literature of Robin Hood, where they do appear they are likely to act on their own behalf and as characters in their own right, rather than primarily as objects of male desire. The notable exception to this is the ballad of 'Robin Hood and Allen a Dale' (first printed in 1663) where Robin's interest is in helping the young man and in rescuing the bride from an unwanted match. Although the scene is missing from the broadside, in the version of this ballad in the Forresters Manuscript,

Robin takes care to make sure that the bride also wants to marry Allen. There are what may be seventeenth-century affectations in 'Robin Hood and Allen a Dale', but it undoubtedly comes from an older original, and an earlier ballad on the theme was known in the late sixteenth century to the writer of the Sloane Manuscript, in which the young bride-groom is William Scarlock and Robin disguises himself as a beggar.

A strikingly different attitude is revealed in the sixteenth-century 'Play of Robin Hood' where Maid Marian appears as a non-speaking part, who is viewed as a possession to be given and received for the sake of male pleasure rather than as an individual in her own right. In this crude, boisterous knockabout of a play, the spirit of Good Yeomanry is reduced to a straightforward show of male virility, and the contrast with the spirit of the ballads and the *Gest* is nowhere more obvious than in its shoddy treatment of the only female character.

'For the love of Our Lady'

Robin's respect for women is closely associated with his reverence for the Virgin Mary. Although living women may be few and far between in early Robin Hood literature where they are cast in largely peripheral roles, Robin's devotion to 'Our Lady' puts a powerful female presence at the heart of the legend. As the object of Robin's devotion, the Virgin Mary is perhaps the most significant woman in the Robin Hood cycle.

Robin treats Mary as a real presence in his world, as someone he can strike a bargain with, someone he trusts absolutely, someone he could never betray. Robin expects the monks of St Mary's Abbey to take a similar attitude to their patron, but they see his straightforward devotion as naïve, and barely pay lip-service to a faith in Mary's intercession in earthly affairs.

The *Gest* and the earliest ballads date from the fifteenth century, and reveal fifteenth-century attitudes to religion. To understand how this might have looked in the thirteenth century, we may turn to the *Cantigas de Santa Maria* which were composed for the Spanish king Alfonso the Wise. There are more than 400 *cantigas*, and each song tells the story of a miracle associated with the Virgin Mary—how she intercedes to save the king's ferret from his horse's hoofs, how she reveals where a stolen piece of meat is hidden, how she strikes down a man who refuses to pay back the money he owes. The absurd homely quality of some of these miracles is deliberate; it is their very improbability which affirms the power of the divine feminine in everyday life. So, while some modern readers might smile at Robin's simplicity in attributing the repayment of his loan to divine intervention, for a medieval reader this could just as easily be understood as a demonstration of the Virgin's genuine intervention through what appears outwardly to be the natural course of events. In the *Gest*, the question is left open, and this ambiguity is deliberate. Tastes had changed, popular religious thought had moved on through preachers such as John Ball and John Wycliff, and the obviousness of miracles in earlier literature was no longer fashionable in a new era.

Robin's steadfast devotion and implicit trust in this female aspect of divine power is always presented as pure and good. It underlies his values and his judgements, and in 'Robin Hood and the Monk' is explicitly invoked as the source of his luck. As Robin is guided by Mary, his men are guided by him, and so the whole band of merry men is guided by Our Lady, which puts an influential female figure in a central role in the medieval legend. It was only after the Protestant Reformation when the cult of Mary fell into in abeyance, that the need for another central female character led to Maid Marian becoming a significant figure in the Robin Hood story.

Places and place names in the Gest and the ballads

As in other early and traditional sources, Robin Hood is associated in the *Gest* both with Nottingham and with Barnsdale in Yorkshire, but the association with Barnsdale is much stronger and, in common with many of the ballads, the *Gest* never mentions Sherwood by name.

Barnsdale crosses the Great North Road to the south of Barnsdale Bar near Wentbridge. It would have been a good spot to intercept passing travellers, and the road was protected here in Roman times by a small fort near what is now Robin Hood's Well. Just to the north of Robin Hood's Well, the Great North Road meets another old Roman road, and the meeting of the two roads was the site of the Bishop's Tree, where Robin Hood is said to have danced with the Bishop of Hereford. The name Watling Street is used locally to refer to the Great North Road (more often called Ermine Street) but might also have been used for the other Roman road now known as Straight Lane. A wood overlooking this spot is named on nineteenth-century maps as Sales Wood and nearby was Sales Quarry, and these place names apparently recall the place named in the *Gest* as 'the Sayles'. If so, the Sayles would have been a useful vantage point for Little John, Much and Will Scarlock to watch over both roads as they do in the *Gest*—another less convincing proposal for the site of the Sayles is at Sayles Plantation just outside Wentbridge. Whereas the poet of the *Gest* was apparently familiar with local geography across much of northern England, even relatively significant places such as Wentbridge may have been unknown to later copyists, causing confusion at II, v.54.

Sir Richard at Lee, the poor knight of the *Gest*, presumably has his home 'at Lee' in Over Wyresdale, Lancashire. This lies outside the Robin Hood heartland, and Holt's identification of 'Verysdale' as Wyresdale has not been universally accepted, but no other English

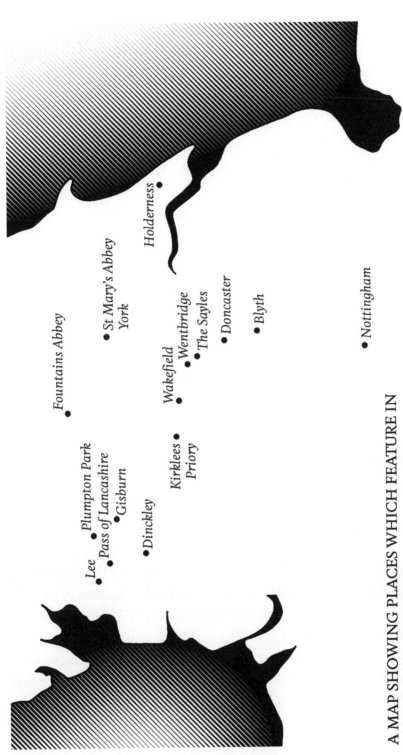

A MAP SHOWING PLACES WHICH FEATURE IN
A GEST of ROBIN HOOD AND EARLY BALLADS

river or dale seems to fit so well philologically (although a possible alternative might be sought in Weardale, Co. Durham). Furthermore, this is not the only reference to this part of Lancashire. In the *Gest*, VII v.4, we read that the king searched for Robin Hood well beyond the limits of Barnsdale:

> Along the Pass of Lancashire
> > He went both far and near,
> But when he came to Plumpton Park;
> > He missed many of his deer.

The high pass known as the Trough of Bowland on the old boundary between Yorkshire and Lancashire, connects the knight's Lancashire home in Wyresdale with the West Riding of Yorkshire. This is the road Sir Richard at Lee would have taken to Barnsdale, and must be the 'Pass of Lancashire' referred to in the *Gest*. Along the same road lies the village of Gisburn, the probable home of Sir Guy of Gisburn in the ballad; this village in the Ribble Valley is now part of Lancashire, but was once in the West Riding of Yorkshire. At nearby Lower Agden in the Forest of Gisburn is a field which is named as Plumpton Park in a tithe award of 1864. A less likely alternative for Gisburn is found at Guisborough, Yorkshire (North Riding) which appears as 'Gysburne' in the charter of Gisborough Abbey, an area which belonged to Robin's cousin, Robert Bruce, Lord of Annandale.

In the same cluster of western locations is the village of Dinckley in the Ribble Valley in Lancashire, which may once have been home to the Sir Roger who helps to kill Robin Hood at Kirklees Priory. The *Gest* names Sir Roger first as 'of Donkesly' (VIII v.35) and then 'of Donkestere' (VIII v.38) and most editors have simply assumed that 'Donkesly' is a mistake for Doncaster. It seems somewhat unlikely however that the well-known place name 'Doncaster' could have been mistakenly rendered as 'Donkesly', and very much more likely that an obscure place name would be mistakenly replaced with a commonly known one. The name 'Donkesly' also carries a rhyme, so it cannot have been miscopied by the fifteenth-century editor and must be original to the verse, whereas the name 'Donkestere' is unrhymed and may be readily emended to 'Donkesly' without damage to the metre or rhyme scheme. Dinckley is about 15 miles by road from Gisburn, home of Sir Guy, and about 30 miles from Wyresdale, home of Sir Richard at Lee. Earlier forms of the place name Dinckley are more similar to the name 'Donkesly' from the *Gest*—it is recorded as 'Dunkythele' in 1246, and 'Dunkedeley' in 1258, and it is thought to be the place name behind the surname Dunkerley.

A note on texts and translations

There is no shortage of scholarly editions which exactly reproduce original sources from the repertoire of Robin Hood ballads, along with learned discussion of their ambiguities. This is not another such edition. My aim is to present good readable (and singable) versions of each ballad or play for the twenty-first century, preserving as much as possible of both the literal sense and the spirit of the original sources in Modern English verse.

The Robin Hood poems are written in rough-and-ready verse which is no stranger to forced rhyme. Dismiss it as doggerel if you like, but it is a perfect fit for these tales of Robin Hood where a more refined style would be out of place. It is not elitist or self-conscious, and that is its charm. It's a style which survives in popular poetry to this day, and to translate it into anything other than the same straightforward hearty style would be to betray the spirit of the original verse, perhaps even the spirit of Robin Hood.

In reworking the English, I've been careful to avoid obvious archaisms such as 'thou' and 'thee' or 'hath' and 'hast', but I haven't always felt the need to straighten out word order to match the rules of modern prose. These poems about our legendary past were never meant to sound up-to-date, and I wanted to preserve something of their old-world charm but without it becoming a barrier to modern readers. The rhythm, especially in the *Gest*, is not always as regular as might be expected, which not only reflects the original sources but is easier on the ear when listening to a long recitation.

Wherever there is more than a single source for a ballad, there are differences between them. I have translated the earliest sources more-or-less directly from the edition *Robin Hood and Other Outlaw Tales* by Knight and Ohlgren (1997) with reference to Dobson and Taylor's *Rymes of Robyn Hood* (1976, 1989) and Nielsen's excellent online edition of the *Gest*. For the later ballads, I have drawn on the wider range of sources in Francis J. Child's classic work, *English and Scottish Popular Ballads* (Vol.III, Part V, 1888) with additional sources where appropriate including Bertrand Bronson's *Traditional Tunes of the Child Ballads* (Vol.III, 1966) and Stephen Knight's edition of the Forresters Manuscript (*Robin Hood: The Forresters Manuscript*, 1998).

Wherever possible, I have drawn most heavily on the oldest text (usually from the Percy Folio) while incorporating readings from other traditional sources where they seem better to me. The Forresters Manuscript has been a particularly useful source, as it preserves complete versions of many texts before they were cut to fit the printed broadside tradition. I have stuck closely to original sources without slavishly following any one specific copy text but, where there are gaps or other difficulties, I have deliberately bridged any missing verses by combining alternative versions and, where necessary, supplying newly 'reconstructed' lines.

I've tried to keep my own additions to a minimum, but I have felt the need to 'restore' more than usual of the ballad of 'Robin Hood's Death'. The earliest text is from the Percy Folio, a manuscript rescued by Bishop Thomas Percy before it was completely torn up by a servant to light fires. Unfortunately, he was too late to save the entire manuscript, and the section where this ballad was written only survives as half pages, so a large part of the original text has been lost. Although more than one complete chapbook version exists, they have dropped key elements of the story as told in the earlier ballad.

The first major gap comes when Robin and John encounter an old woman kneeling on a plank over a stream, and ends with what may or may not be the same character giving Robin something 'To give to Robin Hood' with the implication that they know he is going to his death. There is no equivalent scene in later versions of the ballad, but the surviving details fit perfectly with the figure of 'the washer at the ford', a traditional death omen known from Scottish, Irish, Welsh and Breton lore, and so this is the role I have given to the old woman in this ballad.

The second major gap comes after Robin has been bled, and immediately before the fight with Red Roger. The character of Red Roger does not appear in the later chapbook versions of the ballad, but he is apparently the same character as Sir Roger of Dinckley (sometimes rendered as 'of Doncaster') who appears in the same role at the end of the *Gest*, so he must have featured in the medieval story. It is possible that the original legend made Red Roger solely responsible for Robin Hood's death by taking advantage of Robin's weakness after medical bleeding to deal his death blow, but I have followed accepted tradition in emphasising the role of the Prioress of Kirklees. Robin's greatest concern when we rejoin the ballad is that he should receive the last rites from a priest before he dies, and we must assume this theme has been introduced in the missing verses. Robin's concern to receive the last rites would have been normal and uncontroversial in pre-Reformation England, but may have been deliberately expunged by later Protestant editors.

The third gap in the manuscript comes as Robin is giving instructions for his burial and takes us to the end of the ballad. Here I have simply supplied verses from later tradition. It is remarkable that not only does Robin apparently die unconfessed, but he asks to be buried with grave goods in the style of a pagan hero. Aside from his continual battles with religious and secular authorities, this may be another feature of Robin Hood's legend that led to its consistent condemnation by churchmen.

In total, I have written an additional twelve verses to fill the gaps in 'Robin Hood's Death', but the missing sections might actually have been somewhat longer. I have also added two blocks of one-and-a-half verses to 'Robin Hood and the Monk' to help the flow of the story; some editors have suspected much larger gaps but these short additions seem to me to be all that is necessary to maintain both the narrative and the verse structure. In both 'Robin Hood and the Monk' and 'Robin Hood and the Potter' I have added occasional half verses to keep the regular pattern of four-line verses.

There is some confusion in the Percy Folio between the texts of 'Robin Hood and Guy of Gisburn', 'Robin Hood and the Monk' (the main text of which is missing from at least the surviving pages of this manuscript) and another ballad of 'Robin Hood and the Butcher' (which reworks the story of 'Robin Hood and the Potter'). The original first verse of 'Guy of Gisburn' is almost identical with the opening verse of 'Robin Hood and the Monk' and is followed by three confused verses in which Robin apparently recounts a dream describing his own capture, to which Little John responds rather too optimistically.

It's difficult to see how this beginning could ever have been intended to lead into the main action of 'Guy of Gisburn' and it seems much more likely that all these verses were originally part of a lost version of 'Robin Hood and the Monk'. If so, this is important evidence that the ballad of 'Robin Hood and the Monk' was widely known and survived into the seventeenth century. These verses also explain Robin's sombre mood at the beginning of the ballad of the Monk— he has had a dream in which he is captured, a dream which will become a self-fulfilling prophecy. Unfortunately, not enough survives of this scene to incorporate it in its proper place in 'Robin Hood and the Monk'. Just as the first verses of 'Guy of Gisburn' belong to the story of the Monk, so the first verses of 'Robin Hood and the Butcher' have no bearing on the story of Robin Hood's encounter with the Butcher but perfectly fit the scenario of 'Robin Hood and Guy of Gisburn' where they properly belong. I have also added two verses based on the opening verses from the play of 'Robin Hood and the Sheriff' which partly mirrors the story of the ballad of Guy of Gisburn.

A word of explanation is needed on my treatment of the ballad which is here called 'Robin Hood and the Old Woman' because my understanding of the history of this text differs from its previous editor. It seems to me that, whereas the Forresters text of 'Robin Hood and the Old Wife' may show touches of a late sixteenth-century or early seventeenth-century hand, it broadly preserves an earlier version of the ballad than the printed text of 'Robin Hood and the Bishop' (Child 143) which has been more thoroughly reworked in the seventeenth century. Aside from its improbable substitution of a bishop in the role of the Sheriff of Nottingham, the printed ballad has the characteristic double rhyme of seventeenth-century printshop productions, and incorporates verses which clearly belong to a longer version of 'Robin Hood and the Bishop of Hereford' (Child 144) which must have told a fuller story similar to the Forresters text of that ballad. The motivation for this reworking may have been partly to make use of verses which had been cut from the abbreviated version of 'Robin Hood and the Bishop of Hereford', and partly that a ballad called 'Robin Hood and the Bishop' was considered more saleable than 'Robin Hood and the Old Wife'. It is not possible to say with certainty whether this ballad has a medieval origin but it is generally in keeping with medieval tradition, and it may be significant that the twelve pence allotted for both stockings and shoes would not have bought a pair of shoes at seventeenth-century prices.

The text of 'Robin Hood and Allen a Dale' is based on both the text of the broadside and on the ballad of 'Robin Hood and the Bride' from the Forresters Manuscript, with reference to the outline of the story as sketched in the sixteenth-century Sloane Manuscript. It seems both the broadside and the Forresters text are descended from a common original which was known to the writer of the Sloane Manuscript, but each has developed the story in a slightly different direction. It would be disingenuous to pretend it is possible to actually recover the lost original ballad but, by bringing the two texts back together under guidance from the Sloane Manuscript, something akin to that original can perhaps be rediscovered.

As well as the three texts of 'Robin Hood's Birth' known to Child, at least two more have been noted in oral tradition, but both are close to Buchan's text which probably circulated as a Scottish broadside during the eighteenth century—its heroine's unlikely name of 'Clementina' must surely have been inspired by the Jacobite queen of that name. Buchan's text has its heroine die in childbirth, but Anna Gordon's version lets her live. In keeping with my overall approach to the ballads, I have chosen whatever lines and verses seem best to reflect what may have been the earliest version of the tradition. I have also looked for parallels elsewhere in ballad tradition, so as to remove some of the literary affectations in Buchan's version. As with 'Robin Hood and Allen a Dale', whilst the resulting ballad may not be a perfect restoration of the lost tradition, it perhaps hints at what that tradition might have been.

Both of the plays were probably originally developed by companies of actors, so the written text is secondary to performance. The first survives in a manuscript from c.1475 which preserves only the dialogue, without any indication of who speaks what line, or indeed who some of the characters are. It involves the Sheriff of Nottingham, Robin Hood and Friar Tuck, as well as an unnamed knight and two unnamed outlaws. The broad outline of the story is clear and the first part is similar to the ballad of 'Robin Hood and Guy of Gisburn', but some of the details have been read in more ways than one. The theme of the medieval play is purely anti-authoritarian, and it invites us to take the side of the outlaws against the repressive interpretation of justice embodied by the sheriff. This contrasts markedly with the jovial spirit of the later play, which shows the new direction Robin Hood's legend would take in coming centuries.

The sixteenth-century 'Play of Robin Hood' was registered by William Copland in 1560, but may be earlier. Other editions of this play, including two influential compendiums of Robin Hood texts (Dobson and Taylor, 1976, and Knight and Ohlgren, 1997) consider the text as two separate plays or 'dramatic pieces' but, although the play clearly divides into two unrelated halves, both halves were surely always intended to be performed together, punctuated by a dance in the middle. If necessary, the two halves could even be played by the same actors, with the actor for Friar Tuck doubling as the Potter, and the actor for Maid Marian doubling as the Potter's boy Jack. So although narrative logic would divide the text into two separate plays, for performance purposes it is a single play, and it would be strange to insist on a division that did not exist in the original publication.

A very suitable song for the dance which separates the two halves of the play survives in two early seventeenth-century medleys of popular songs, 'New Fashions' by William Cobbold (1560-1639) and 'A round of three Country Dances in one' by Thomas Ravenscroft (1590-1633). Words and music in the two versions are similar but not identical, suggesting the original song had probably been well known for decades or even generations, and local variants had developed. I have included the words of both versions here, and the music can be found in Appendix E.

The two halves of the play are based loosely on the ballads of 'Robin Hood and the Curtal Friar' and 'Robin Hood and the Potter'. The printed text of the play is in fact earlier than the earliest surviving text of 'The Curtal Friar', but some form of the ballad was probably among the 'rhymes of Robin Hood' which had been sung for generations before, and the outline of the story is broadly similar. There are more differences between the play's second half and the related ballad of 'Robin Hood and the Potter'. In the play, the potter has a boy called Jack who doesn't appear in the ballad, and there is no hint that Robin will take the Potter's place in Nottingham, which forms the central story of the ballad; instead Little John steps up to defeat the Potter in a Robin-meets-his-match narrative.

Copland describes the 'Play of Robin Hood' as 'a new play for to be played in May Games', but it seems unlikely that this was a genuinely 'new' and original work. The ending of the second half is very confused in Copland's text, where the Potter offers to pay Robin Hood with half of his possessions before Robin even asks for payment, whereupon he refuses to pay him a penny. This cannot be right, and

I have reordered the speeches to restore sense, adding a few extra lines modelled closely on the ending of the first part. Very probably, Copland got his text for the play from a performer, and the lines were copied down out of order. It's almost impossible to imagine how the writer of a 'new play' could have made a similar mistake.

Although only the words now survive, they suggest an action-based physical performance. Spectators might have remembered the '*Deus hic!*' gag (where Friar Tuck disguises his drunken hiccups as pious Latin) but they'd certainly have remembered how Robin gets up on the Friar's back, and the Friar throws him in the 'water'; they'd have remembered the fight scenes, which could have been excitingly choreographed; they'd have remembered Robin smashing Jack's pots on the ground, and they'd have remembered the dancing. In the context of all this action, the written text drops into the background.

Overall, although I have sometimes had to make significant interventions in somewhat problematic original texts, I have always tried to restore rather than reimagine, drawing on alternative versions for the best reading, and any additional material is as minimal as possible whilst remaining as close as possible to what must have been lost. My hope is that these restorations will allow the ballads, songs and plays to sing again in a form that is truer to the original poems and songs than a more exact reproduction of the surviving sources could achieve.

Timeline

c.1208	–	Robin Hood is born
1209	–	Margaret of Huntingdon marries Alan of Galloway
1216	–	Nine-year-old Prince Henry succeeds his father John as King Henry III of England
1217	–	The Charter of the Forest attempts to re-establish free men's rights in the royal forest
1219	–	David, Earl of Huntingdon, dies, and is succeeded by his son John
1223	–	Dervorguilla of Galloway marries John de Balliol
c.1223-24		Robin Hood reputedly attacks a party of foresters
1225	–	Robertus Hood listed as a fugitive
	–	King Henry III reissues Magna Carta and the Charter of the Forest
1227	–	King Henry III comes of age and begins to rule in his own right
1232	–	Randolf, Earl of Chester, dies
	–	Richard Marshall rebels against Henry III because the king has failed to abide by charters issued in 1225
1237	–	John, Earl of Huntingdon, dies, and the Honour of Huntingdon is divided between his sisters
1239	–	Prince Edward (later King Edward I) is born
1240	–	Peter de Aigueblanche is installed as Bishop of Hereford
1258	–	A council of English barons takes control of government and enacts reforms in the Provisions of Oxford and Ordinance of the Sheriffs
	–	Simon de Headon first appointed as Sheriff of Nottingham
1259	–	The Provisions of Westminster extend the reforms of the Provisions of Oxford
c.1260-62		Robertus Hod is among the robbers of Saero de Gargrave in Holderness during local disturbances against the king

TIMELINE

1261	–	King Henry III repudiates the Provisions of Oxford and Westminster
	–	John de Balliol first appointed as Sheriff of Nottingham
1262	–	Simon de Warwick, Abbot of St Mary's, is forced to flee the city of York
1263	–	Simon de Montfort leads the barons against the king and takes control of government
1264	–	After his defeat at the Battle of Lewes, the captive King Henry III agrees the Mise of Lewes establishing government by council and parliament
1265	–	Simon de Montfort calls England's first representative parliament
	–	Simon de Montfort is killed at the Battle of Evesham
1266	–	Robertus Hod and his son Roger are among rebels on the Isle of Ely
	–	According to chronicler Walter Bower, 'Robertus Hode was now banished…'
1267	–	Simon de Headon is succeeded as Sheriff of Nottingham by his son Gerard
1268	–	John de Balliol dies
	–	Peter de Aigueblanche dies
1270	–	Simon de Warwick begins a lavish rebuilding programme at St Mary's Abbey, York
1272	–	Prince Edward succeeds his father Henry as King Edward I of England
1283	–	King Edward I summons the Parliament of Acton Burnell on a similar basis to Simon de Montfort's Parliament of 1265
	–	According to chronicler Andrew Wyntoun, Robin Hood flourished at this time
c.1288	–	Supposed date for Robin Hood's death, based on Bower and the *Gest*
c.1294–99		According to an anonymous annotation in a copy of Higden's *Polychronicon*, Robin Hood flourished 'around this time'

A GEST OF
ROBIN HOOD

I

Stop and listen, everyone
   That comes of freeborn blood;
I'll tell you of a good yeoman,
   His name was Robin Hood.

Robin was a bold outlaw,
   When once he walked this ground;
Such a courteous outlaw as he was then
   May never again be found.

Robin stood in Barnsdale,
   And leaned against a tree,
And beside him there stood Little John,
   A good yeoman was he.

And also there was good Scarlock,
   And Much, the miller's son;
There wasn't an inch of his whole body
   But it was worth a man.

Then out spoke Little John
   And said to Robin Hood,
'Master, if you'd dine on time,
   It would do you much good.'

Then out spoke good Robin:
   'I have no wish to eat,
Until I find some bold baron,
   Or unknown guest to greet.

'I first must meet some baron bold
   That can pay for the best,
Or else some knight or squire,
   That lives here in the west.'

A good custom had Robin then
   In whatever place he was,
That every day before he dined,
   Three times he would hear Mass.

The first was for God the Father,
   The next for the Holy Ghost,
The third was for Our dear Lady,
   That he did love the most.

Robin so loved Our dear Lady
   That, for fear of deadly sin,
He would never harm the company
   That any woman was in.

'Master,' then said Little John,
   'As we must set our table,
Tell us first where we must go,
   To lead what life we're able.

'Where we must take, where we must leave,
   Where we must stay behind,
Where we must rob, where we must steal,
   Where we must beat and bind.'

'It matters not,' then said Robin,
   'We shall do well, I vow,
If we never harm the husbandman,
   That labours with his plough.

'Neither shall you harm the good yeoman
   That walks by the green wood's end,
Nor any knight nor any squire
   That would be a good friend.

'But as for bishops and archbishops,
   You shall them beat and bind,
And the high Sheriff of Nottingham,
   You shall keep him in mind.'

'We'll learn this well,' said Little John,
   'This lesson we'll repeat,
But it's late in the day; God send us a guest,
   So that we soon may eat!'

'Take your good bow in your hand,' said Robin,
   'And take Much for company,
And also William Scarlock,
   No man shall stay with me.

'And walk up to the Sayles,
   And so to Watling Street,
And wait there for some unknown guest,
   That you may chance to meet.

'Be he an earl or any baron,
   Abbot, knight or squire,
Bring him to me at the lodge;
   His dinner I'll prepare.'

They went up to the Sayles,
   These yeomen all three,
But they looked east, and they looked west,
   And no one could they see.

But as they looked towards Barnsdale,
   There did they see a knight,
Riding along a hidden path,
   And he was a sorry sight.

All mournful was his countenance,
   And gone was all his pride,
His one foot in the stirrup stood,
   The other waved beside.

His hood hung down into his eyes,
   He rode in simple style;
There was never a more wretched man
   That rode a sorrier mile.

Little John was most courteous,
   And went down on his knee:
'You are welcome, gentle knight;
   You're welcome here to me.

'You're welcome to the green wood,
   Noble knight and free;
My master has awaited you, sir,
   Fasting for hours three.'

'Who is your master?' said the knight.
   John said, 'Robin Hood.'
'He is a good yeoman,' said the knight,
   'Of him I've heard much good.

'I'll agree,' he said, 'to go with you,
   My brothers, by your side,
Though my plan was to have dined this day
   At Doncaster or Blyth.'

They set forth with this gentle knight;
   His face was worn with care,
And from his eyes across his cheeks,
   Ran many a bitter tear.

They brought him then to the lodge door—
   When Robin did him see,
He courteously took off his hood
   And went down on his knee.

'Welcome, Sir Knight,' then said Robin.
   'You're welcome here to me;
I have waited for you, sir,
   Fasting for hours three.'

The gentle knight then answered him,
   With words both fair and free:
'May God keep you, good Robin,
   And all your company.'

They washed their hands and dried them,
   And both sat down to eat;
They had bread and wine in plenty,
   And venison for meat.

Swans and pheasants they had the best,
   And wildfowl for their food;
They lacked not for any little bird
   That ever lived in the wood.

'Enjoy your meal, Sir Knight,' said Robin.
   'I thank you, sir,' said he,
'I haven't had such a dinner as this
   In all these past weeks three.

'If I come again, Robin,
  Here through this country,
I shall make you as good a dinner
  As you have made for me.'

'I thank you, knight,' said Robin,
  'For whenever my dinner I get;
I was never so hungry, by merciful God,
  That I begged for my dinner yet.

'But pay before you go,' said Robin,
  'I think it only right;
It was never the custom, by merciful God,
  For a yeoman to pay for a knight.'

'I have nothing in my coffers,' said the knight,
  'That I may give, to my shame.'
'Little John, go look,' said Robin,
  'And don't dally, for fear of blame.

'Tell me the truth,' then said Robin,
  'As God your judge may be.'
'I have no more than ten shillings,' said the knight,
  'May God judge over me.'

'If you have no more,' said Robin,
  'I will not take one penny,
But I will gladly lend you more,
  If you have need of any.

'Step forward, Little John,' he said,
  The truth now tell to me,
If there is only ten shillings,
  Or if there's more to see.'

Little John spread out his mantle
　Carefully on the ground,
And there he found in the knight's coffers
　No more than half a pound.

Little John left it where it lay,
　And to his master drew.
'What news now, John?' said Robin.
　'Sir, the knight has spoken true.'

'Pour out the best of wine,' said Robin,
　'The knight shall first begin;
It's very strange, it seems to me,
　That your clothing is so thin.

'Tell me one thing,' said Robin,
　'And a secret it shall be—
You must have been made a knight by force,
　Or else through yeomanry,

'Or else you have been a poor husband,
　That lived in trouble and strife,
A usurer or philanderer,' said Robin,
　'That has led a wrongful life.'

'I am none of those,' said the knight,
　'By God that I hold dear,
But my ancestors have all been knights
　For more than a hundred year.

'But it can happen that a man
　May suffer loss and pain,
Yet God who reigns in heaven above
　May raise him up again.

'Within these last two years,' he said,
    'As my neighbours well can say,
Four hundred pounds in good money
    I readily could pay.

'Now I have nothing,' said the knight,
    'As God did so ordain,
Except for my children and my wife,
    Till God restore it again.'

'How did it happen,' said Robin,
    'That you lost your property?'
'Through my great folly,' said the knight,
    'And for my family.

'I had a son indeed, Robin,
    That should have been my heir,
When he was twenty winters old,
    To joust was his desire.

'He slew a knight of Lancaster
    And a squire bold,
And so to save him in his right
    My goods were pawned and sold.

'My lands were pledged in hock, Robin,
    Until a certain day,
To a rich abbot hereabouts
    Of St Mary's Abbey.'

'What is the sum?' said Robin,
    'And how much is the fee?'
'Sir,' he said, 'four hundred pounds;
    The abbot gave to me.'

'So, if you lose your lands,' said Robin,
　'What will you do then?'
'I'll sail the salt sea,' said the knight,
　'And not come back again.

'I'll see where Christ was crucified,
　On the mount of Calvary,
So farewell friend, good day to you;
　It may no better be.'

Salt tears fell from both his eyes;
　He would have gone his way.
'Farewell friend, good day to you;
　I have no more to pay.'

'Where are your friends?' said Robin.
　'Sir, no one wants to know me,
Though when I was rich enough before
　Good fellowship they'd show me.

'Yet now they run away from me,
　Just like the startled deer,
And they take no more heed of me
　Than if I wasn't there.'

For pity then wept Little John,
　Scarlock and Much did too;
'Pour out the best of wine,' said Robin,
　'It's the least that we can do.

'But do you have no friend,' said Robin,
　'Who'll stand as surety?'
'I have none,' then said the knight,
　'But for God who died on tree.'

'Don't play the fool,' then said Robin,
   'I won't have that at all;
Do you think I'd ask God for surety,
   Or St Peter, or St Paul?

'Nay, by Him that did me make,
   And shaped both moon and sun,
Find better surety,' said Robin,
   'Or money you'll get none.'

'I have no other,' said the knight,
   'Who'd help me with my debt,
Unless it be Our dear Lady—
   She never failed me yet.'

'By merciful God,' said Robin,
   'Though I search all England round,
There is no better surety
   That ever could be found.

'Step forward, Little John,' he said,
   'And go to my treasury,
And bring to me four hundred pounds,
   And count it well for me.'

Then Little John stepped forward,
   And Scarlock went before;
He counted out four hundred pounds
   By eighteen and two score.

'Can this be right?' asked little Much;
   John said, 'Never you mind!
It goes to help a gentle knight,
   Who has fallen on hard times.

'Master,' then said Little John,
  'His clothing is very thin;
You must give the knight a livery,
  To clothe his body in.

'For you have scarlet cloth and green, master,
  And many a rich array;
There is no merchant in merry England
  So rich, I dare well say.'

'Cut him three yards of each colour,
  And measure it well for me.'
Little John took no other measuring rod
  But the length of his bow tree.

And at every handful he measured out
  He jumped along three feet.
'Such a devil's draper,' said little Much,
  'I never yet did meet!'

Scarlock looked at him and laughed,
  And said, 'By God Almighty,
John may give him good measure,
  Because it costs him so lightly.'

'Master,' then said Little John
  To gentle Robin Hood,
'You must give the knight a horse,
  To carry home these goods.'

'Fetch him a grey courser,' said Robin,
  'And a saddle new.
He is Our Lady's messenger;
  God grant that he be true.'

'And a good palfrey,' said little Much,
  'To maintain him in his right.'
'And a pair of boots,' said Scarlock,
  'For he is a gentle knight.'

'What would you give him, Little John?' said Robin.
  'Sir, a pair of golden spurs,
To pray for all this company,
  God save him from his cares.'

'When shall my day be?' said the knight,
  'And where shall my payment be?'
'In twelve months from today,' said Robin,
  'Under this greenwood tree.

'It would be a great shame,' said Robin,
  'For a knight alone to ride,
Without a squire, yeoman, or page,
  To walk by his side.

'I'll lend you Little John, my man,
  For he shall be your squire,
And he'll take the yeoman's place for you,
  Whenever you desire.'

II

Now the knight has gone on his way:
  His fortune he thought good,
And when he looked at Barnsdale
  He blessed bold Robin Hood.

And when he thought of Barnsdale,
  Of Scarlock, Much, and John,
He blessed them for the best company
  That ever he came on.

Then out spoke that gentle knight,
  To Little John he did say,
'Tomorrow I must go to York,
  To St Mary's Abbey.

'And to the abbot of that place
  I must pay four hundred pounds;
Unless I'm there before tonight
  I shall lose all my lands.'

The abbot said to his convent,
  As he walked around the grounds,
'Twelve months ago there came a knight
  Who borrowed four hundred pounds.

'He borrowed it against his lands,
  As he did then request;
Unless he comes this very day
  He shall be dispossessed.'

'It is still early,' said the prior,
   'The day is not yet far spent;
I'd rather pay a hundred pounds,
   Than lose such lands and rent.'

'The knight is far across the sea,
   In England's cause to fight;
He's wracked with hunger and with cold,
   And many a sleepless night.'

'It would be shameful,' said the prior,
   'To take his land that way;
Though you may have no conscience,
   You do him wrong this day.'

'You're always in my beard,' said the abbot,
   'By St Richard of Chichester!'
Then in there came a fat-headed monk,
   Who was high cellarer.

'He's either dead or hanged,' said the monk,
   'By God that I hold dear,
And we shall have his wealth to spend—
   Four hundred pounds a year.'

The abbot and high cellarer
   So brazenly went on,
The courts of justice thereabouts
   This lord abbot did run.

The chief justice and many more
   Had taken on their hands
Every debt the knight had owed,
   To cheat him of his lands.

They judged the knight unfairly,
  This abbot and all the rest:
'Unless he comes this very day
  He shall be dispossessed.'

'He will not come,' said the chief justice,
  'I dare well undertake.'
But to the sorrow of them all
  The knight came to the gate.

Then out spoke that gentle knight
  To all his company:
'Now put on your simple clothes
  That you wore upon the sea.'

Then they put on their simple clothes,
  And to the gates they came;
The porter was ready waiting,
  And welcomed them all the same.

'Welcome, Sir Knight,' said the porter.
  'My lord is dining now
Along with many a gentleman
  Who are here for the sake of you.'

The porter swore a mighty oath,
  'By God that did make me,
This is the very best gift horse
  That ever I did see!

'Lead the horses to the stable,' he said,
  'Where they may rested be.'
'They shall not go there,' said the knight,
  'By God who died on tree!'

Lords were sitting down to dine
　There in the abbot's hall;
The knight went in and kneeled down,
　And he did greet them all.

'Be glad, Sir Abbot,' said the knight,
　'I've come to keep my day.'
The first word that the abbot spoke was,
　'Have you brought my pay?'

'Not one penny,' said the knight,
　'By God that did make me.'
'You're a wicked debtor' said the abbot.
　'Sir Justice, drink to me!

'Why are you here,' said the abbot,
　'If you haven't brought your pay?'
'To beg in God's name,' said the knight,
　'That you'll wait till another day.'

'The day has come,' the justice said,
　'On your lands I must foreclose.'
'Now, good Sir Justice, be my friend,
　And defend me from my foes!'

'I'm paid by the abbot,' said the justice,
　'Both in clothes and fee.'
'Now, good Sir Sheriff, be my friend!'
　'Nay, by God!' said he.

'Now, good Sir Abbot, be my friend,
　In your benevolence,
And keep my lands within your hand
　Till I make recompense!

'And I will be your faithful servant,
  And serve you faithfully,
Until you have four hundred pounds
  In money for your fee.'

The abbot swore a mighty oath,
  'By God that died on tree,
Go get yourself what land you can,
  But you'll get none from me.'

'By merciful God,' then said the knight,
  'That all this world has made,
If I can't get my land again,
  I swear I'll be well paid.

'May God, that was of a maiden born,
  Grant we shall succeed!
For it is good to test a friend
  To see if he's true indeed.'

The abbot angrily stared at him,
  And rudely he did call:
'Out!' he said, 'You false knight!
  Now get out of my hall!'

'You lie!' then said the gentle knight,
  'Abbot, in your hall;
No false knight I ever was,
  By God that made us all!'

Then up stood that gentle knight,
  And to the abbot said he,
'When you leave a knight to kneel so long,
  You show no courtesy.

'In jousting and in tournament
    Far and wide I've been,
And put my life as much at stake
    As any man I've seen.'

'What more can you give,' said the justice,
    'So the knight will make a release?
Or else I think I can safely say,
    You'll not hold your land in peace.'

'A hundred pounds,' said the abbot.
    The justice said, 'Give him two.'
'Nay, by God!' said the knight,
    'You shall not get it so.

'Though you should give a thousand more,
    You'll never be the buyer;
No heir of mine shall ever be
    An abbot, justice or friar!'

He dashed across to a side table,
    It was a table round,
And there he shook out from his bag
    A straight four hundred pound.

'Here take your gold, Sir Abbot,' he said,
    'Which you lent me before;
If you'd been courteous to me now,
    I would have given more.'

The abbot sat still, and ate no more
    Of all his royal fare;
He shook his head on his shoulders,
    With his eyes fixed in a stare.

'Give me back my gold,' said the abbot,
  'Sir Justice, that I gave you.'
'Not a penny,' said the justice,
  'By God that I hold true.'

'Sir Abbot, and you men of law,
  Now I have kept my day;
Now I shall have my land again,
  No matter what you say.'

The knight dashed out through the door,
  And cast off all his care,
And he put on his good clothing,
  And left the simple clothes there.

He went out singing merrily,
  As men have told in tale;
His lady met him at the gate,
  At home in Wyresdale.

'Welcome, my lord,' said his lady.
  'Sir, have you lost your goods?'
'Be merry, my lady,' said the knight,
  'And pray for Robin Hood,

'That ever his soul may be in bliss,
  For he helped me in my need;
Had it not been for his kindness,
  We would be beggars indeed.

'The abbot and I are now agreed,
  And he has got his pay;
The good yeoman lent it to me,
  As I came along the way.'

This knight lived happily at home,
   The truth for to say.
Till he had got four hundred pounds,
   All ready for to pay.

He provided himself with a hundred bows,
   The strings were fitted fine,
A hundred sheaves of good arrows
   With heads that brightly shine;

And every arrow a yard in length,
   With peacock-feather flights;
The nocks were made of white silver—
   It was a splendid sight.

He provided himself with a hundred men,
   All harnessed in armour bright,
And he himself in that same band,
   And clothed in red and white.

He held a lancegay in his hand,
   And with a happy song,
And another man to carry his bags
   To Barnsdale rode along.

But at Wentbridge there was a wrestling match,
   And so he tarried there,
For the best yeomen in the West Riding
   Had come from far and near.

A splendid game had been set up
   For the prize of a white bull,
And a courser with saddle and bridle
   Beset with burnished gold.

A pair of fine gloves, a golden ring,
   A cask of wine besides;
And whoever bore himself the best
   Would bear away the prize.

There was a yeoman in that place,
   And he had won the game,
But because he was a stranger there,
   He was to have been slain.

The knight took pity on this man,
   In the wrestling ring where he stood;
He said that yeoman should not be harmed,
   For love of Robin Hood.

The knight with all his hundred men,
   He pushed into the ring,
With bows bent and arrows sharp,
   To shame that gathering.

They all stood back and made him room,
   To hear what he would say;
He took the yeoman by the hand,
   And said he'd won the day.

He gave him five marks for his wine,
   Which sat before them there,
And said it should be opened then,
   For everyone to share.

So long as this gentle knight stayed there
   Until that sport was done,
So long was Robin waiting and fasting,
   For three hours after noon.

III

Stop and listen, everyone,
    All you who now are here,
Of Little John, that was the knight's man,
    A good tale you shall hear.

It was upon a merry day
    When young men went to shoot,
That Little John fetched down his bow,
    And said he would them meet.

Three times Little John shot about,
    And he always split the wand;
The proud Sheriff of Nottingham
    By the target marks did stand.

The sheriff swore a mighty oath:
    'By Him that died on tree,
This man is the best archer
    I ever yet did see.

'Tell me now, my brave young man,
    What is now your name?
In what place were you born,
    And where do you call home?'

'In Holderness, sir, I was born,
    In truth, as I may tell;
Men call me Reynold Greenleaf
    At home where I do dwell.'

'Tell me, Reynold Greenleaf,
  Would you dwell with me?
And every year, I'll give you
  Twenty marks as your fee.'

'I have a master,' said Little John,
  'And a courteous knight is he,
But if you could get leave of him,
  Then better it may be.'

The sheriff got for Little John
  Twelve months as his leave,
For which he gave him right away
  A good horse and a brave.

Now Little John is the sheriff's man—
  God grant us our desire!
But Little John kept thinking how
  To repay him for his hire.

'By almighty God,' said Little John,
  'And by my true loyalty,
I shall be the worst servant to him
  That ever yet had he.'

It fell upon a Wednesday
  The sheriff was hunting gone,
And Little John was left behind,
  And lay on his bed at home.

And so he lay there fasting
  Until the afternoon.
'Good Sir Steward, I beg you,
  Bring me my dinner,' said John.

'It is too much for Greenleaf
    To keep so long a fast,
And so I beg you, Sir Steward,
    To bring me my repast.'

'You'll neither eat nor drink,' said the steward,
    'Until my lord comes back.'
'I vow to God,' said Little John,
    'I'll give your head a crack!'

The butler was most discourteous,
    Where he stood on the floor;
He rushed off to the buttery
    And bolted fast the door.

Little John gave the butler such a knock
    His back nearly broke in two;
Though he should live for a hundred years,
    He'd be the worse for that blow.

John kicked the door in with his foot;
    It opened well and fine,
And there he took a good helping,
    Both of ale and of wine.

'If you won't dine,' said Little John,
    'I'll give you something to drink,
And though you may live for a hundred winters,
    On Little John you'll think.'

Little John ate, and Little John drank,
    As long as he had need,
But the sheriff had a cook in his kitchen,
    That was a bold man indeed.

'I make a vow to God,' said the cook,
  'Of servants you're the worst,
That thus you should your hunger slake,
  Or thus you quench your thirst.'

And there he struck at Little John
  Three blows, as I hear tell;
'I make a vow to God,' said Little John,
  'These blows do please me well.

'You seem a bold and daring man,
  The kind I like the best,
And before I get out of this place
  I'll put you to the test.'

Little John drew a good bright sword,
  The cook he took another;
They had no thought to turn and flee,
  But boldly fought together.

They fought each other all about
  For half an hour and more;
Neither could do the other harm,
  In the space of a whole hour.

'I make a vow to God,' said Little John,
  'And by my true loyalty,
That you are one of the best swordsmen
  I ever yet did see.

'If you could shoot as well with a bow,
  You'd come to the green wood with me,
And twice in every year your clothes
  Would be new livery,

'And every year from Robin Hood
　You'd have twenty marks as your fee.'
'Put up your sword,' said the cook,
　'And comrades we shall be.'

Then he fetched for Little John,
　The sweetbreads of a deer;
With the best of bread, and the best of wine,
　They drank and made good cheer.

And when they both had drunk their fill,
　They gave their word, each one,
That they would be with Robin Hood
　Before the night was done.

They went as fast as they could go,
　Straight to the treasure hall;
The locks made from the best of steel,
　They broke them one and all.

They took away the silverware,
　And all that they could get;
Dishes, drinking bowls and spoons,
　Not one did they forget.

They took more than three hundred pounds,
　In good coins that were there,
And to Robin Hood in the green wood,
　They straightway did it bear.

'God save you, my dear master,
　May Christ your watchman be!'
And Robin then said to Little John,
　'You're welcome here to me.'

'And so is that fair yeoman
    That you've brought here with you;
What is the news from Nottingham?
    Little John, tell me true.'

'The proud sheriff sends you greeting,
    And sends to you here by me
His cook and all his silverware,
    And three hundred pounds and three.'

'I make a vow to God,' said Robin,
    'And by the Trinity,
It was never of his own free will
    That he sent these things to me.'

A thought then came to Little John
    About a cunning ruse;
Through the forest he ran five miles,
    And it turned out as he'd choose,

For there he met the proud sheriff,
    Hunting with horn and hound;
Little John kept his courtesy,
    And kneeled down on the ground.

'God save you, my dear master,
    May Christ watch over you!'
'Reynold Greenleaf!' said the sheriff,
    'Where have you been just now?'

'I've been all through this forest,
    And a fair sight I did see;
It was one of the fairest sights
    That was ever yet shown to me,

'For there I saw the fairest stag,
  His colour is of green,
And seven score deer are in the herd
  That with him may be seen.

'Their antlers are so sharp, master,
  Of sixty tines, I'd say,
That I didn't dare to shoot at them
  For fear they would me slay.'

'I make a vow to God,' said the sheriff,
  'That's a sight I'd like to see!'
'Hurry then, my dear master,
  And come along with me.'

The sheriff rode, and Little John
  On foot he didn't lag,
And when they came to Robin, he said,
  'Look, sir, here's the master stag!'

The proud sheriff stood still in his stirrup,
  A sorrowful man was he:
'Woe betide you, Reynold Greenleaf,
  That you have now betrayed me.'

'I make a vow to God,' said Little John,
  'Master, you are to blame,
Because I was kept from my dinner
  When I was with you at home.'

Soon the sheriff was set to his supper,
  And served with silver bright,
But when he saw his own silverware,
  For sorrow he could not eat.

'Cheer up, Sheriff,' said Robin Hood,
  'And have no fear of strife,
And for the love of Little John,
  I'll let you keep your life.'

When they had drunk and eaten well,
  And the day was at a close,
Robin commanded Little John to take
  The sheriff's shoes and hose,

His tunic and his jacket,
  That was well furred and fine,
And to fetch for him a green mantle,
  To wrap his body in.

Robin commanded his bold young men,
  Under the greenwood tree,
That they lie down, dressed just the same,
  Where the sheriff might them see.

The proud sheriff lay there all night
  In his underwear and shirt,
Which is not strange in the green wood,
  But his sides began to hurt.

'Cheer up now,' said Robin Hood,
  'Sheriff, for charity,
For indeed, this is our custom,
  Under the greenwood tree.'

'Your custom is harder,' said the sheriff,
  'Than any hermit or friar;
For all the gold in merry England
  I wouldn't want to live here.'

'All this twelve months,' said Robin,
  'You shall live here with me,
And I'll teach you, proud sheriff,
  An outlaw for to be.'

'Before I stay another night,' said the sheriff,
  'Robin, I beg of you,
Cut off my head tomorrow instead,
  And I forgive it you.

'Let me go,' said the sheriff,
  'For the love of almighty God,
And I will be the best friend
  That ever yet you had.'

'You must swear me an oath,' said Robin,
  'By the bright sword in my hand,
That you shall never do me harm,
  By water or by land.'

'And if you find any of my men,
  By night or yet by day,
Upon your oath, you must swear
  To help them if you may.'

Now the sheriff he has sworn his oath,
  And homewards he began;
He'd had as much of the green wood
  As ever he could stand.

IV

The sheriff lived in Nottingham
  And was glad to get away,
While Robin and his merry men
  In the green wood still did stay.

'Let's have our dinner,' said Little John.
  Robin Hood said, 'Nay,
For I fear Our Lady must be cross with me,
  As she hasn't returned my pay.'

'Have no doubt, master,' said Little John,
  'For the sun is not yet set;
I dare well say and safely swear,
  The knight will prove true yet.'

'Take your bow in your hand,' said Robin,
  'And take Much for company,
And also William Scarlock,
  No man shall stay with me.

'And walk up to the Sayles,
  And so to Watling Street,
And wait there for some unknown guest,
  That you may chance to meet.

'Whether he be a messenger,
  Or one that makes good cheer,
If he should be a poor man,
  With him my goods I'll share.'

So Little John went off then,
   Half in rage and wrath,
With a good sword buckled underneath
   His mantle of green cloth.

They went up to the Sayles,
   These yeomen all three,
But they looked east, and they looked west,
   And no one could they see.

But as they looked towards Barnsdale,
   Along the highway side,
They spied two monks all dressed in black,
   Who did each on a palfrey ride.

Then up spoke Little John,
   To Much he did say,
'I dare to bet upon my life,
   These monks have brought our pay.

'So cheer up then,' said Little John,
   'And check your bows of yew,
And be sure your hearts are steady and strong,
   Your bowstrings trusty and true.

'This monk has fifty two yeomen
   And seven pack horses stout;
There is no bishop in all this land
   So royally rides about.

'Brothers,' said Little John,
   'We number only three,
But unless we can bring these monks to dinner,
   Our master we dare not see.

'Bend your bows,' said Little John,
  'Make all that crowd to stand;
The life and death of the foremost monk
  I hold within my hand.

'Stop, wretched monk!' said Little John,
  'I order you to stand,
And if you move, by merciful God,
  Your death is in my hand.

'And bad luck on your head,' said Little John,
  'Right under your hat band,
For you have made our master cross,
  He's had to wait so long.'

'Who is your master?' said the monk.
  Little John said, 'Robin Hood.'
'He is a wicked thief,' said the monk,
  'Of him I've heard no good.'

'You're lying,' then said Little John,
  'And you'll be sorry in time;
He is a yeoman of the forest,
  Who has asked you to dine.'

Much stood by with a broad arrow,
  That he took from his bow;
He set the point to the next monk's breast,
  And swiftly laid him low.

Of the fifty two brave young yeomen
  There remained not one,
Except for a page boy and a groom,
  To lead the horses with Little John.

They brought the monk to the lodge door,
  Whether or not he would,
Although it was much against his will,
  To speak with Robin Hood.

Robin pushed his hood back,
  So the monk could see his face;
The monk was not so courteous,
  But left his hood in place.

'He's uncouth, master, by merciful God,'
  Little John said then.
'It matters not,' said Robin,
  'But courtesy he has none.

'How many men,' said Robin,
  'Did this monk have now, John?'
'He had fifty two when first we met,
  But most of them are gone.'

'Blow a horn,' said Robin,
  'So fellowship we may know.'
Then seven score of bold yeomen
  Came running all in a row.

And every one wore a good mantle
  Of scarlet fine and new,
And they all came to good Robin,
  To know what they should do.

They made the monk to wash himself,
  And then sit down to eat,
Both Robin Hood and Little John
  Then served him with his meat.

'Enjoy your meal, monk,' said Robin.
   'I thank you, sir,' said he.
'What is your abbey? Who is your saint?
   And where might your abbey be?'

'St Mary's Abbey,' said the monk,
   'But I am humble there.'
'In what office?' said Robin,
   'Sir, the high cellarer.'

'You're all the more welcome,' said Robin,
   'As welcome you may be.
Pour out the best of wine,' said Robin,
   'This monk shall drink to me.

'But I've been wondering,' said Robin,
   'The whole of this long day,
I fear Our Lady is cross with me,
   As she hasn't returned my pay.'

'Don't doubt her, master,' said Little John,
   'You have no need to fear;
This monk has come from her own abbey,
   And has brought your pay, I'll swear.'

'Our Lady stood as surety,' said Robin,
   'Between a knight and me,
For a little money I lent to him,
   Under the greenwood tree.

'If you have brought that silver here,
   I beg you let me see,
And I shall help you afterwards,
   If you have need of me.'

This monk was in a sorry state,
    A mighty oath he swore,
'Of this surety you speak about,
    I never heard before.'

'I make a vow to God,' said Robin,
    'You are to blame, I know—
For, as God was always a righteous man,
    His mother is also.

'You told me with your own tongue,
    You cannot now say nay,
You said you are her servant,
    And serve her every day.

'And you've been made her messenger,
    My money for to pay;
Therefore I thank you all the more
    You've come upon your day.

'What's in your coffers?' said Robin,
    'Truly to me tell.'
'Sir,' he said, 'just twenty marks,
    As I hope to live well.'

'If there's no more,' said Robin,
    'I won't take a penny from you,
And if you have need of any more,
    I'll lend that to you too.

'But if I find there's more,' said Robin,
    'I'll take it as my own,
Except for your spending money, monk,
    Of that I will take none.

'Step forward, Little John,' he said,
  The truth now tell to me,
If there is only twenty marks,
  Or if there's more to see.'

Little John spread his mantle down,
  As he had done before,
And he counted out from the monk's coffer
  Eight hundred pounds and more.

Little John left it where it lay,
  And to his master went he;
'This monk, sir,' he said, 'is honest enough,
  Our Lady has doubled your fee.'

'I make a vow to God,' said Robin,
  'What did I just tell you?
Our Lady is the truest woman
  That ever yet I knew.

'By merciful God,' said Robin,
  'Though I search all England round,
There is no better surety
  That ever could be found.

'Pour the best of wine! Let him drink,' said Robin,
  'A toast to your Lady so kind,
And if she ever has need of Robin Hood,
  A friend she shall him find.

'And if she has need of any more money,
  Come here again to me,
And, by this token that she has sent,
  For each penny I'll pay back three.'

The monk was bound for London,
    In council there to go,
About that knight who rode so high,
    And how to bring him low.

'Where are you going?' said Robin.
    'To our manors and our farms,
To reckon with our bailiffs,
    That have done us much harm.'

'Step forward, Little John,' he said,
    And hear what I do tell;
I know no yeoman who can search,
    A monk's coffers so well.

'How much is on the other horse?' said Robin,
    'The truth we must now see.'
'By Our Lady,' then said the monk,
    'Have you no courtesy?

'To ask a man to dinner,
    And then to rob him blind!'
'It's our custom of old,' said Robin,
    'To leave but little behind.'

The monk set his spurs to his horse's side,
    No longer would he stay.
'Have a drink,' then said Robin,
    'Before you ride away.'

'Nay, by God,' then said the monk,
    'I'm sorry I ever came here;
I could have eaten for much less
    In Blyth or Doncaster.'

'Greet your abbot from us,' said Robin,
    'And your prior too, I pray,
And ask him to send a monk like you
    To dine with me every day.'

Now let us leave that monk a while,
    And speak about the knight,
For he was still coming to keep his day,
    While it was still light.

He headed straight to Barnsdale,
    Under the greenwood tree,
And there he found Robin Hood,
    And the merry company.

The knight got down from his good palfrey,
    When Robin he did see;
He courteously pushed back his hood,
    And got down on his knee.

'God save you, Robin Hood,
    And all this company.'
'You are welcome, gentle knight,
    And right welcome to me.'

Then out spoke good Robin Hood,
    To that knight so free:
'What brings you to the green wood?
    I pray you, sir knight, tell me.

'And welcome you are, gentle knight,
    Why have you been so long?'
'Because the abbot and the chief justice
    Wanted to take my land.'

'Have you got your land again?' said Robin,
  'Come tell it to me true.'
'Aye, by God,' said the knight,
  'For which I thank God and you.

'But don't take it badly,' said the knight.
  'That I have been so long,
For I helped a poor yeoman at wrestling,
  When the judges had done him wrong.'

'Nay, by God,' said Robin,
  'Sir Knight, I thank you for this;
Whoever may help a good yeoman,
  My friendship shall be his.'

'Take this four hundred pounds,' said the knight,
  'Which you once lent to me,
And here is another twenty marks
  As thanks for your courtesy.'

'Nay, by God,' then said Robin,
  'Keep it for another day,
For Our Lady, by her cellarer,
  Has sent to me my pay.

'And if I were to take it twice,
  The shame would be on me,
But truly, gentle knight,' he said,
  'You're welcome here to me.'

When Robin had told his tale,
  He laughed and made good cheer.
'Upon my word,' then said the knight,
  'I have your money here.'

'Spend it well,' said Robin,
  'My gentle knight so free,
And you are welcome, gentle knight,
  Under my trestle tree.

'But what are all these bows for?'
  And these feathered arrows too?'
'By God,' then said the knight,
  'A poor present for you.'

'Step forward, Little John,' said Robin,
  And go to my treasury,
And bring me the four hundred pounds
  The monk has overpaid me.

'Take this four hundred pounds,
  My gentle knight and true,
And buy a horse and harness good,
  And gild your spurs anew.

'And if you're short of money to spend,
  Come to Robin Hood,
And by my word, you shan't go short,
  While I have wealth and goods.

'And be sure to spend the four hundred pounds,
  Which I have given you,
And don't keep yourself so thriftily,
  As you were wont to do.'

So did good Robin help the knight,
  To live without such woe;
May God, who sits in heaven above,
  Grant that we all live so!

V

Now the knight has taken his leave,
  And he went upon his way,
While Robin Hood and his merry men
  Lived quietly for many a day.

Stop and listen, everyone,
  And hear what I shall say,
How the proud Sheriff of Nottingham
  Announced a game to play,

That all the best archers of the north
  Should come upon a day,
And he that shoots the best of all
  Shall bear the prize away.

He that shoots the best of all,
  The farthest, straight and good,
At a pair of fair targets,
  Under the green wood,

The finest arrow he shall win,
  Its shaft of silver white,
Its head and feathers of rich red gold,
  In England there's none the like.

Good Robin came to hear of this,
  Under his trestle tree:
'Get ready then, my brave young men;
  That shooting I will see.

'Prepare yourselves, my merry young men,
  You shall come with me too,
And I will test the sheriff's good faith,
  To see if his word is true.'

When they had their bows well bent,
  Their arrows straight and good,
There were seven score of brave young men
  That stood by Robin Hood.

And when they came to Nottingham,
  The range was long and fair;
Many was the bold archer
  That shot with a strong bow there.

'Only six men shall shoot with me;
  The rest of you take heed,
And stand by with your good bows bent,
  To see I am not deceived.'

The fourth outlaw to bend his bow,
  Was none but Robin Hood,
With the proud sheriff looking on,
  As he by the targets stood.

Three times did Robin shoot about,
  And always split the wand,
As likewise did good Gilbert
  With the White Hand.

Little John and good Scarlock
  Were archers good and fair;
Little Much and good Reynold,
  No worse than many there.

But when they all had shot about,
　These archers fair and good,
Evermore the very best,
　Indeed was Robin Hood.

They gave to him the finest arrow,
　For he was the best with bow;
He took the gift so courteously,
　And to green wood he would go.

They shouted out at Robin Hood,
　And great horns began to blow:
'A curse on treason!' said Robin,
　'You're most evil to know.

'And a curse upon you, proud sheriff,
　If that's how you'd treat me;
It's not what you once promised me
　Under my trestle tree.

'If I had you again in the green wood,
　Under my trestle tree,
You'd leave me with a better pledge
　Than your true loyalty.'

Full many a bow then was bent,
　And arrows they let glide;
Many a tunic there was rent,
　And wounded many a side.

The outlaws' shooting was so strong
　That none could drive them back,
And so the proud sheriff's men,
　They fled away full quick.

Robin saw the ambush start,
   And wished it might not be;
Many an arrow there was shot
   Among that company.

Little John was wounded sore,
   With an arrow in his knee,
So he could neither walk nor ride;
   It was a great pity.

'Master,' then said Little John,
   'If ever you loved me,
And for the sake of Our Lord's love
   That died upon the tree,

'And as the reward for serving you,
   For service that I gave,
Never let the proud sheriff
   Take me now alive.

'But draw out your shining sword,
   And so strike off my head,
And give me wounds both deep and wide,
   So that you leave me dead.'

'I could not wish,' said Robin,
   'John, that you were dead,
For all the gold in merry England,
   If it lay here outspread.'

'God forbid,' said little Much,
  'That died upon the tree,
That you should ever, Little John,
  Part from our company.'

He took him up upon his back,
  And carried him a long mile;
Many a time he laid him down,
  To shoot again awhile.

There was then a fair castle,
  A little within the wood;
A double ditch lay all about,
  High walls around it stood.

And there lived that good gentle knight,
  Sir Richard at the Lee,
That Robin had lent four hundred pounds,
  Under the greenwood tree.

Sir Richard took good Robin in,
  And all his company:
'You are welcome, Robin Hood;
  You're welcome here to me.

'I heartily thank you for your help,
  And for your courtesy,
And also for your great kindness,
  Under the greenwood tree.

'There is no man in all this world
  To me who is so dear,
And despite the proud Sheriff of Nottingham,
  You shall be sheltered here.

'Shut the gates, draw up the bridge,
  Let no one in at all,
But arm yourselves and make ready,
  And go to man the wall.

'For one thing, Robin, I promise you,
  By God who died on tree,
These forty days you may stay here,
  To drink and eat with me.'

Tables were laid, and cloths were spread
  At once, in double time,
So Robin Hood and his merry men
  They all sat down to dine.

VI

Stop and listen, everyone,
   And hearken to my song,
How the proud Sheriff of Nottingham,
   And men of arms strong

Came quickly to the high sheriff,
   To stir up the countryside,
And they beset the knight's castle,
   Around the walls outside.

The proud sheriff loudly shouted out,
   And said, 'You traitor knight,
You're harbouring the king's enemies,
   Against his law and right.'

'Sir, I freely own that I have done
   These deeds as you indict,
By all the lands that I possess,
   As I am a true knight.

'Be gone, sirs, on your way,
   And do no more to me
Until you know our king's will,
   Whatever it may be.'

So the sheriff had his answer,
   Without any lying,
And he went on to London town,
   To go and tell our king.

There he told him of that knight,
   Likewise of Robin Hood,
And also of the bold archers,
   That were so noble and good.

'He will confess to what he has done,
   To maintain that outlaw band;
He wants to be lord without heed of you,
   Across the whole northland.'

'I'll be at Nottingham,' said our king,
   'Within this next fortnight,
And I will take this Robin Hood,
   And so I will that knight.

'Go home now, Sheriff,' said our king,
   'And do as I command,
And gather enough good archers,
   From all across the land.'

The sheriff has taken his leave,
   And went upon his way,
And Robin Hood to the green wood went,
   Upon a certain day.

And Little John was healed of the arrow
   That had wounded his knee,
And he went straight to Robin Hood,
   Under the greenwood tree.

Robin Hood walked in the forest,
   Under the leaves of green—
For the proud Sheriff of Nottingham,
   That was a grief and pain.

The sheriff failed there with Robin Hood,
　　He could not take his prey,
So he watched for this gentle knight,
　　Both by night and day.

He kept watch on the gentle knight,
　　Sir Richard at the Lee,
Who went hawking by the riverside,
　　To watch his hawks fly free.

There he caught this gentle knight,
　　With his strong-armed band,
And carried him off to Nottingham,
　　Bound both foot and hand.

The sheriff swore a mighty oath,
　　By Him that died on Rood,
He'd rather than a hundred pounds
　　That he had Robin Hood.

The knight's wife chanced to hear this,
　　A lady fair and good;
She mounted on a fine palfrey,
　　And rode to the green wood.

When she came into the forest,
　　Under the greenwood tree,
There she found Robin Hood,
　　And all his company.

'May God bless you, good Robin,
　　And all your company,
And for Our dear Lady's sake,
　　Grant this boon for me.

'Never let my wedded lord
   Be shamefully slain, I pray;
He is caught and bound for Nottingham,
   For the love of you, this day.'

Straightaway, good Robin said
   To that lady so free,
'What man has taken your lord away?'
   'The proud sheriff,' said she.

'The sheriff has carried him off,' she said,
   'Indeed as I do say,
But he has not yet gone three miles
   So far upon his way.'

Then up jumped good Robin,
   Like a mad man he was:
'Get ready now, my merry men,
   For Him that died on the Cross.

'And whoever forsakes this sorrow,
   By Him that died on the Tree,
No longer in the green wood
   Shall he live here with me.'

Their good bows soon they bent there,
   Seven score or more;
They stopped for neither hedge nor ditch
   That was them before.

'I make a vow to God,' said Robin,
  'The sheriff I will see,
And if I can get hold of him,
  Avenged I will be.'

And when they came to Nottingham,
  They walked along the street,
And soon with the proud sheriff
  Indeed they chanced to meet.

'Stop, you proud sheriff!' he said,
  'Stop, and tell me true,
For some news about our king
  I want to hear from you.

'In seven long years, by merciful God,
  I've not gone so fast on foot,
And I make a vow to God, proud sheriff,
  It is not for your good.'

Robin took a broad arrow,
  And set it to his bow,
And he has shot the proud sheriff
  And quickly laid him low.

And before he could get up again,
  Upon his feet to stand,
Robin cut off the sheriff's head
  With the bright sword in his hand.

'Lie there now, you proud sheriff,
    An ugly sight in death!
No one could ever trust you
    As long as you drew breath.'

His men drew out their shining swords,
    That were so sharp and bright,
And set upon the sheriff's men,
    And put them all to flight.

Robin ran up to that knight,
    And quickly cut his bonds,
He told him to come along with them,
    And put a bow in his hands.

'Leave your horse behind you,
    And learn how to run;
You'll come with me to the green wood,
    Through mire, moss, and fen.

'You'll come with me to the green wood,
    Without any lying,
Until such time as I get us grace
    From Edward, our comely king.'

VII

The king has come to Nottingham,
  With knights in great array,
For to take that gentle knight
  And Robin Hood, if he may.

He asked the men of that country
  About Robin Hood,
And also about that gentle knight,
  Who was so bold and good.

When they had told to him their tale,
  Our king did understand,
And swiftly seized then for himself
  All of the knight's land.

Along the Pass of Lancashire
  He went both far and near,
But when he came to Plumpton Park,
  He missed many of his deer.

Where our king used once to see
  Great herds throughout the wood,
He could hardly find a single stag
  With antlers that were good.

The king grew very angry then,
  And swore by the Trinity,
'I wish that I had Robin Hood,
  Standing in front of me.

'And whoever cuts the knight's head off,
   And brings it here to me,
Can have the lands of that false knight,
   Sir Richard at the Lee.

'I'll give them with my charter,
   And seal it with my hand,
To have and hold for evermore,
   In all merry England.'

Then up spoke an honest knight,
   That in his heart was true:
'O my liege lord and king,' he said,
   'A word I must say to you.

'There is no man in this country
   That could keep that knight's land,
While Robin Hood may ride or walk,
   And carry a bow in his hand.

'Unless you'd have him lose his head,
   The best ball in his hood,
Give it to no one, my lord and king,
   If you wish him any good.'

In Nottingham our comely king
   Then stayed for half a year;
Of Robin Hood or where he lived,
   No word could he hear.

But always good Robin went
   By valley and by hill,
And always slew the king's deer,
   And took them at his will.

Then up spoke a proud forester,
    That stood by our king's knee:
'If you want to see good Robin,
    You must be ruled by me.

'Take five of the best among the knights
    That you have in your ranks,
And go down by the abbey,
    And dress yourselves as monks.

'And I will be your leader,
    And I will lead the way,
And before you come to Nottingham,
    My head I dare to lay

'That you shall meet with good Robin,
    If he is still alive;
And before you come to Nottingham,
    You'll see him with your eyes.'

Our king and five of his best knights,
    Full hastily were dressed,
Each one put on a monk's habit,
    And set out in great haste.

Our king stood tall, above his cowl
    A broad hat on his crown,
He looked just like an abbot,
    As they rode through the town.

Stout boots our king had on,
    Indeed, as I do say;
He rode singing to the green wood,
    And his monks were clothed in grey.

His baggage and his pack horses
  Behind them followed on,
Till deep into the green wood,
  A long mile they had gone.

There they met with good Robin,
  Standing in their way,
And with him was many a bold archer,
  Indeed, as I do say.

Robin took the king's horse,
  Hastily by the rein,
And said, 'Sir Abbot, by your leave,
  A while you must remain.

'We are yeomen of this forest,
  Under the greenwood tree;
We live upon our king's deer,
  No other living have we.

'And you have churches and rents too,
  And gold in great plenty;
Give us some of your money,
  For holy charity.'

Then out spoke our comely king,
  And straightaway said he,
'I brought no more to the green wood
  Than forty pounds with me.

'I've been with our king in Nottingham
  This past fortnight and more,
And on many a great nobleman,
  I've spent much of my store.

'So I have only forty pounds,
  No more than is my due,
But if I had a hundred pounds,
  I'd offer half to you.'

Then Robin split the forty pounds,
  That was all the abbot had;
Half he gave to his merry men,
  And told them to be glad.

Most courteously did Robin say,
  'Your change, sir, I do bring.
May we meet again another day.'
  'I thank you,' said our king,

'But Edward greets you well, our king,
  And sends to you his seal,
And bids you come to Nottingham,
  To share both meat and meal.'

He took out the broad seal,
  And swiftly let him see;
Robin knew his courtesy,
  And went down on his knee.

'I love no man in all the world
  As well as I do my king;
Welcome is my lord's seal,
  And you, for the news you bring,

'Sir Abbot, for the news you bring,
  Today you must dine with me,
For the love that I have for my king,
  Under my trestle tree.'

He led forth our comely king,
  By the hand most fair;
Many a deer was swiftly slain,
  And was made ready there.

Robin took a great big horn,
  And loudly did he blow;
Seven score of brave young men
  Came ready in a row.

They all kneeled down upon their knees,
  Before Robin full fair;
The king said softly to himself,
  And to himself did swear,

'Here is a seemly sight, by God,
  That is both fair and fine,
His men are more at his bidding
  Then my men are at mine.'

Full swiftly was their meal prepared,
  To dinner they have gone;
They served our king with all their heart,
  Both Robin and Little John.

Straightway before our king was set
  The fatted venison,
The good white bread, the good red wine,
  The ale fine and brown.

'Make good cheer,' said Robin,
  'Abbot, for charity,
And for this news that you have brought,
  Blessed may you be.

'Now before you leave us here,
  You must see the life we lead,
So that you may inform our king,
  When you together meet.'

Then up they jumped and, all in haste,
  They drew their bows full fast;
Our king was never so terrified,
  He thought his life was lost.

Two stakes then there were set up,
  And to them they have gone;
By fifty paces, said our king,
  The distance was too long.

On each stake was a rose-garland,
  Where they shot at the post;
'Whoever misses the garland,' said Robin,
  'His arrow shall be lost,

'He must give it to his master,
  Though it be never so fine,
For no man will I spare,
  As I drink ale or wine.

'And he'll take a buffet to his head,
  Which he must leave bare.'
And all that fell to Robin's lot,
  He struck them very sore.

Twice did Robin shoot about,
  And always split the wand,
As likewise did good Gilbert
  With the White Hand.

Little John and good Scarlock,
    For nothing would they spare,
But when they missed the garland,
    Then Robin struck them sore.

At the last shot that Robin shot,
    Before all his friends there,
His arrow missed the garland,
    By three fingers and more.

Then out spoke good Gilbert,
    And thus he did say:
'Master,' he said, 'your tackle is lost;
    Step up, and take your pay.'

'If it be so,' said Robin,
    'It may no better be,
Sir Abbot, I give you my arrow,
    I pray you, sir, serve me.'

'It ill befits my order,' said our king,
    'Robin, by your leave,
For me to strike a good yeoman,
    In case I should him grieve.'

'Strike on boldly,' said Robin,
    'I give you ample leave.'
Straightway our king, on hearing that,
    He rolled up his sleeve,

And he gave Robin such a buffet,
  He nearly felled him there.
'I make a vow to God,' said Robin,
  'You are a sturdy friar.

'There's such strength in your arm,' said Robin,
  'I'm sure you can shoot a bow.'
Thus our king and Robin Hood
  They did each other know.

Robin beheld our comely king
  Keenly in the face,
As did Sir Richard at the Lee,
  And kneeled down in that place.

And so did all the wild outlaws,
  When they saw them kneel:
'My lord, the King of England,
  Now I know you well.'

'Mercy then, Robin,' said our king,
  'Under your trestle tree,
For your goodness and your grace,
  Towards my men and me!'

'Aye, by God,' said Robin,
  'And also, God me save,
I ask your mercy, my lord and king,
  And for my men I crave.'

'Aye, by God,' then said our king,
　'To that I will agree,
If you will leave the green wood,
　With all your company,

'And come home, sir, to my court,
　And there dwell with me.'
'I make a vow to God,' said Robin,
　'And right so shall it be.

'I will come with you to your court,
　Your service for to see,
And bring with me of my men
　Seven score and three.

'But unless your service pleases me,
　'I will come back full soon,
And I'll shoot again at the dun-brown deer,
　As I have always done.'

VIII

'Have you any green cloth,' said our king,
   'That you will now sell me?'
'Aye, by God,' said Robin,
   'Thirty yards and three.'

'Robin,' said our king,
   'Do this now for me,
Sell me some of that cloth,
   For me and my company.'

'Aye, by God,' then said Robin,
   'Or I would be a fool;
Another day you will clothe me,
   I trust, in time for Yule.'

The king cast off his cowl then,
   A green garment he put on,
And so likewise had every knight
   Another hood full soon.

When they were clothed in Lincoln green,
   They cast away their grey:
'Now we shall go to Nottingham,'
   And so our king did say.

Their bows they bent, and forth they went,
   Shooting all in a row,
Towards the town of Nottingham,
   As outlaws they did go.

Our king and Robin rode together,
   Indeed, as I you say,
And they shot a game of pluck buffet,
   As they went along the way.

And many a buffet our king has won
   From Robin Hood that day,
And Robin didn't spare our king
   When giving him his pay.

'God help me,' said our king,
   'I cannot win, I fear;
I couldn't win a shot from you,
   Though I shot all this year.'

All the people of Nottingham
   They stood there and beheld,
And they could see nothing but mantles of green
   That covered all the field.

Then every man to each other did say,
   'I fear our king is slain,
For Robin Hood has come to town,
   Who never let life remain.'

They hastily began to flee,
   Both the yeomen and the knaves,
And old wives that could hardly walk,
   They hobbled on their staves.

The king then laughed aloud at that,
   And called them back instead;
When they saw it was our comely king,
   Indeed they were full glad.

They ate and drank and made merry,
  And joyful songs did sing;
Then to Sir Richard at the Lee
  Out spoke our comely king.

He gave him back his lands again,
  A good man he bade him be;
Robin thanked our comely king,
  And went down on his knee.

But when Robin had lived in the king's court
  For just twelve months and three,
Then he had spent a hundred pounds,
  And all of his men's fee.

In every place where Robin went
  His money he laid down,
Both for knights and for squires,
  To get him great renown.

And when the year was all but gone
  He had no men but two,
Little John and good Scarlock,
  Along with him to go.

Robin saw some young men shoot
  At archery one day;
'Alas!' then said good Robin,
  'My wealth is wasted away.

'Once I was an archer good,
  Who stood both staunch and strong;
I was accounted the best archer
  That was in merry England.

'Alas!' then said good Robin,
  'Alas!' then he did sigh,
'If I live any longer with the king,
  For sorrow I must die.'

Away then went Robin Hood
  Till he came to our king:
'My lord, the King of England,
  Grant me this one thing.

'I made a chapel in Barnsdale,
  That seemly is to see,
It is for Mary Magdalene,
  And that's where I long to be.

'I might never in these seven nights
  Have time to sleep a wink,
Nor ever in these seven days
  Neither eat nor drink.

'I'm longing sore for Barnsdale,
  I wish that I were there;
Barefoot will I make my way
  With a woollen shirt to wear.'

'If it be so,' then said our king,
  'It may no better be,
For seven nights I give you leave,
  No longer, to part from me.'

'I thank you, lord,' then said Robin,
  And went down on his knee;
He took his leave most courteously;
  To the green wood then went he.

And when he came to the green wood,
　Upon a merry morning,
There he heard the little notes
　Of birds' merry singing.

'It is so long,' said Robin,
　'Since I last was here;
I'd like a little while to shoot
　At the dun-brown deer.'

Robin slew a great big stag,
　His horn he then did blow,
So all the outlaws of that forest
　That horn they would know,

And they all gathered together,
　As fast as they could go;
Seven score of brave young men
　Came ready in a row.

And gladly they took off their hoods,
　And went down on one knee;
'Welcome,' they said, 'our master,
　Under this greenwood tree.'

Robin lived in the green wood,
　For twenty years and two;
For dread of our King Edward,
　Away he would not go.

And yet he was deceived, indeed,
　Through a wicked woman's sin,
The prioress of Kirklees,
　That was of his close kin,

All for the love of a knight,
  Sir Roger of Dinckley,
That was her own beloved—
  May bad luck on them be!

Together they took their counsel
  Robin Hood to slay,
How best they might do that ill deed,
  His murderers to be.

Then out spoke good Robin,
  In that place where he stood,
'Tomorrow I'll go to Kirklees,
  To be skilfully let blood.'

Sir Roger of Dinckley,
  By the prioress he lay,
And there they betrayed good Robin Hood,
  Through their false play.

May Christ who died upon the Cross
  Have mercy on Robin Hood,
Because he was a bold outlaw,
  Who did poor people good.

BALLADS OF ROBIN HOOD

Robin Hood's Birth

There's many that speak of grass, of grass,
   And many that speak of corn,
And many that sing of Robin Hood
   But know little where he was born.

His father was an earl's steward,
   That served for meat and fee;
His mother was Earl Huntingdon's daughter,
   A lady fair and free.

When her nine months were near at end,
   And eight months they were gone,
This lady's cheeks with tears were wet,
   Her face was pale and wan:

'Oh, narrow is my gown, Willie,
   That was wont to be so wide,
And gone is all my fair colour,
   That was wont to be my pride.

'And if my father should get word
   That you have lain with me,
Before he either eats or drinks,
   He'll hang you from a tree.

'But shall we go to my mother's bower,
   That stands upon the green?
Or shall we go to the good green wood,
   Where we may not be seen?'

'I will not go to your mother's bower,
   That stands upon the green,
But let's go to the good green wood,
   Where we may not be seen.'

He took his good sword by his side,
   His buckler and his bow,
He took his lady by the hand,
   To the green wood they did go.

With slowly steps this couple walked,
   Two miles but scarcely three.
Till when this lady's pains came on,
   She lay down beneath a tree.

'Oh, had I a bunch of red rowans,
   To cheer my heart again,
And had I but a good midwife,
   To ease me of my pain!'

'I'll bring you a bunch of red rowans,
   To cheer your heart again,
And I'll be to you a good midwife,
   To ease you of your pain.'

'Get far away from me, Willie,
  For that may never be;
It was never the use of our country,
  And it won't be used by me.

'Go, take your good sword by your side,
  Your buckler and your bow,
And you may go through the good green wood
  To hunt the buck and doe.

'You will stay in the good green wood,
  And with the chase go on,
Until a white hind pass you by,
  Then straight to me you'll come.'

He took his good sword by his side,
  His buckler and his bow,
And he went through the good green wood,
  To hunt the buck and doe.

When night was gone and day came on,
  And the sun began to peep,
Up rose the Earl of Huntingdon
  Out of his drowsy sleep.

He called upon his merry young men
  By one, by two, by three:
'Oh, what's become of my daughter dear,
  That she hasn't come in to me?

'I dreamed a doleful dream last night,
  God grant it come to good!
For I dreamed I saw my daughter dear
  Drown in the salt sea flood.'

They sought her here, they sought her there,
  They sought her up and down,
They sought her in the good green wood,
  Where Willie and she had gone.

Where in the green wood Willie strayed,
  And chased the deer and game,
Until the white hind passed him by,
  Then to his love he came.

He took his good sword by his side,
  Fast through the wood went he,
And there he found his own true love,
  Beneath the green oak tree.

But he looked east, and he looked west,
  To see what could be spied,
He saw the Earl of Huntingdon,
  And many men beside.

The earl with all his company,
  Came through the woods so wild,
And there he saw his daughter dear,
  Nursing a little child.

He took the little boy in his arms,
  And kissed him tenderly;
Said, 'Though I would your father hang,
  Your mother's dear to me.'

He kissed him over and over again:
  'My grandson here I claim,
And Robin Hood in the good green wood,
  That shall be his name.'

So, there's many that speak of grass, of grass,
  And many that speak of corn,
And many that sing of Robin Hood
  But know little where he was born.

It was not in the hall, the hall,
  Nor in the painted bower,
But it was in the good green wood,
  Among the lily flower.

Robin Hood and the Foresters

Earl Randolf kept Robin for fifteen winters,
Derry, derry down,
Until he was fifteen years old,
And Robin grew into a big fellow,
Of courage stout and bold.
Hey down, derry, derry down.

Robin Hood he went to fair Nottingham,
In an alehouse for to dine;
There he was aware of fifteen foresters,
Who were drinking ale and wine.

'What news? What news?' said bold Robin Hood;
'What news would you like to know?
Our king has provided a shooting match,
And I'm ready with my bow.'

'We hold it in scorn,' then said the foresters,
'That ever a boy so young
Should bear a bow before our king,
That's not able to draw bowstring.'

'Don't call me a boy,' said Robin Hood,
'Though my youth I can't deny,
For if you want to test my strength,
On the ground I'll make you lie!'

Then forward stepped a forester
  And he wrestled Robin sore,
But Robin struck with his heels so high
  And he threw him to the floor.

But then up spoke the forester,
  'Although you may wrestle well,
Yet to draw a bow as befits a man,
  In that you have no skill.'

'I'll bet you twenty marks,' said bold Robin Hood,
  'By the leave of Our Lady,
That I shall strike down yonder stag,
  Two hundred yards from me.'

'You're on, you're on!' said the foresters,
  'We'll take your money free,
You can't hit the stag at two hundred yards,
  Nor can you make him die.'

Robin Hood he bent a noble bow,
  And a broad arrow he let fly,
On the stag's near side he broke two ribs,
  On the far side he broke three.

His arrow being sharp and keen,
  Right through the buck did fly,
And by the strength of Robin's arm,
  Stuck fast into a tree.

The stag did skip, and the stag did leap,
  And the stag fell to the ground.
'The wager is mine,' said bold Robin Hood,
  'If it were for a thousand pound.'

'The wager's none of yours,' then said the foresters,
    'Although you may be in haste;
Take up your bow, and away you go,
    Or else your sides we'll baste.'

Robin Hood he took up his noble bow,
    And his broad arrows the same,
And Robin Hood he laughed and began to smile,
    As he went over the plain.

Then Robin Hood he bent his noble bow,
    And his broad arrows he let fly,
Till fourteen of these fifteen foresters
    Upon the ground did lie.

He that did this quarrel first begin,
    Went running over the plain,
But Robin Hood he bent his noble bow,
    And he fetched him back again.

'You said I was no archer,' said Robin Hood,
    'But now again say so.'
With that he sent another arrow
    That split his head in two.

'You have found me an archer,' said Robin Hood,
    'And your wives may weep for you,
And wish that you never had spoken the word
    That I could not draw a bow.'

The people that lived in fair Nottingham
    Came running out over the plain,
Thinking to have taken bold Robin Hood,
    With the foresters that were slain.

The one that was the fastest afoot,
   Caught up with him where he stood,
But Robin Hood took up his noble bow,
   And he went to the merry green wood.

They carried these foresters into fair Nottingham,
    Derry, derry down,
  Where many did them know;
They dug them graves in the churchyard there,
   And they buried them all in a row.
    Hey down, derry, derry down.

Robin Hood and
the Curtal Friar

In summer time, when leaves grow green,
    And flowers are fresh and gay,
Robin Hood and his merry men
    They went to sport and play.

Then some would leap, and some would run,
    And some would use archery:
'Which of you best can draw a strong bow,
    A good archer to be?

'Which of you can kill a buck?
    Who can kill a doe this day?
Or who can kill a fine fat stag,
    Five hundred foot away.'

Will Scarlock he has killed a buck,
    Much killed a doe that day,
And Little John killed a fine fat stag,
    Five hundred foot away.

'God bless you, John,' said Robin Hood,
    'That you shoot so straight and true;
I would ride my horse for a hundred miles,
    To find one who could match with you.'

That caused Will Scarlock for to laugh,
    He laughed full heartily:
'There's a curtal friar in Fountains Dale
    Who'll beat both you and he.

'That curtal friar in Fountains Dale,
    Well can he draw a bow;
He'll beat you and your best bowmen,
    Though you set them all in a row.'

Then Robin Hood swore a solemn oath,
    It was by St Mary,
That he would neither eat nor drink
    Till the friar he did see.

Robin Hood put on his harness good,
    On his head a cap of steel,
With sword and buckler by his side,
    And they became him well.

He took his good bow in his hand,
    It was made of a trusty tree,
With a sheaf of arrows at his belt,
    And to Fountains Dale went he.

He hid his men in a brake of fern,
    Not far from that nunnery;
Says, 'If you hear my little horn blow,
    Then look you come to me.'

When Robin came to Fountains Dale,
    No further would he ride,
There he was aware of the curtal friar,
    Walking by the waterside.

A pair of black breeches the friar wore,
  On his head was a cap of steel,
With a bright sword and a broad buckler,
  And they became him well.

'I am wet and weary,' said Robin Hood,
  'Good fellow, as you may see;
Will you bear me over this wild water,
  For sweet St Charity?'

The friar took Robin Hood on his back,
  Deep water he did bestride,
And spoke neither a good word nor a bad,
  Till he came to the other side.

But when he came over that wild water,
  He drew his sword of steel:
'Bear me back again, bold outlaw,' he said,
  'Or the sword's edge you shall feel.'

Robin Hood took the friar on his back,
  Deep water he did bestride,
And spoke neither a good word nor a bad,
  Till he came to the other side.

The friar leapt lightly from Robin Hood's back;
  Robin Hood said to him again,
'Bear me back again now, curtal friar,
  Or it shall bring you pain.'

The friar took Robin Hood on his back,
  And stepped in up to the knee;
Till he came to the middle of the stream,
  Neither good nor bad spoke he.

But when he came to the middle of the stream,
   There he threw Robin in:
'Now choose, now choose, my fine fellow,
   Whether you will sink or swim.'

Then Robin Hood swam to a bush of broom,
   The friar to a willow wand;
Bold Robin went dripping onto the shore,
   And took his bow in hand.

One of his best arrows under his belt
   At the friar he let fly;
The curtal friar, with his steel buckler,
   He put that arrow by.

'Shoot on, shoot on, my fine fellow,
   Shoot on as you have begun;
If you shoot here for a summers day,
   Your mark I shall not shun.'

Robin Hood shot very well,
   Till his arrows all were gone;
They took their swords and steel bucklers,
   And fought with might and main.

From ten o' clock they fought that day,
   Till four in the afternoon;
Then Robin Hood went down on his knee,
   To beg of the friar a boon.

'A boon, a boon,' said Robin Hood,
   'I beg it on my knee;
Give me leave to set my horn to my mouth,
   And to blow loud blasts three.'

'That will I do,' said the curtal friar,
  'Of your blasts I have no doubt,
And I hope you blow your horn so hard
  That both your eyes fall out!'

Robin Hood put his horn up to his mouth,
  And he blew loud blasts three;
Soon half a hundred good bowmen,
  Came running over the lea.

'Whose men are these,' said the curtal friar,
  'That come so hastily?'
'These men are mine,' said Robin Hood,
  'They're here to fight for me.'

'As I granted a boon,' said the curtal friar,
  'You may grant this boon for me,
To set my fist against my mouth,
  And to hoot long hoots three.'

'Hoot on, hoot on,' said Robin Hood,
  'Hoot on and never still;
It is not the hooting of a friar's fist
  That can do me any ill.'

The friar put his fist up to his mouth,
  A loud hoot he did blow;
Then half a hundred good guard dogs
  Came running all in a row.

'Here's for every man a dog,' said the friar,
  'And myself for Robin Hood.'
'Nay, by my faith,' said Robin Hood,
  'That will never come to good.

'Now God forbid,' said Robin Hood,
    'That ever I should so do;
I'd rather be matched against two of your dogs
    Before I'd be matched with you.'

Two dogs at once set on Robin Hood,
    One behind and the other before,
And Robin Hood's mantle of Lincoln green
    From off his back they tore.

'Call off your dogs,' then said Little John,
    'Friar, do as I say!'
'Whose man are you,' said the curtal friar,
    'That comes here to babble away?'

'I am Little John, Robin Hood's man,
    Friar, I will not lie;
If you don't call off your dogs very soon,
    Both you and they shall die.'

'Call off your dogs,' said Robin Hood,
    'And you and I may agree;
Call off your dogs, good friar,' he said,
    'And keep good Yeomanry.'

Little John had a good bow in his hand,
    And he shot with might and main;
Soon half a score of the friar's dogs
    Lay dead upon the plain.

The friar he put his fist to his mouth,
    A loud hoot he did blow;
The dogs they couched down every one,
    They couched down in a row.

'Hold your hand, good fellow,' said the curtal friar,
    'Your master and I will agree,
And we will have new orders taken
    With all the haste that may be.

'What is it you want, bold outlaw?' he said,
    'Have done, and tell it me.'
'That you should go to the merry green wood,
    And there remain with me.

'If you will forsake deep Fountains Dale,
    And forsake fair Fountains Abbey,
Then every Sunday throughout the year,
    In gold I'll pay your fee,'

This curtal friar had kept Fountains Dale
    For seven long years or more;
There was never a knight, nor a lord, nor an earl
    That could make him yield before.

Robin Hood and the
Pinder of Wakefield

In Wakefield there lives a jolly pinder,
  In Wakefield, all on a green,
  In Wakefield, all on a green.

'There's neither knight nor squire,' said the pinder,
  'Nor baron that is so bold,
Dare take a ramble to the town of Wakefield,
  But he pays a pledge to the pinfold.'

All this was heard by three bold young men,
  It was Robin Hood, Scarlock, and John;
With that they did see the jolly pinder,
  As he sat under a thorn.

'Now, turn again, turn again,' said the pinder,
  'For a wrong way have you gone,
For you have strayed from the king's highway,
  And made a path over the corn.'

'Ah well, that's a great shame,' said jolly Robin,
  'As there's three of us, and you're just one.'
The pinder leapt back then thirty good foot;
  It was three good foes against one.

He set his back against a thorn,
  And his foot against a stone,
And there he fought for a long summer's day,
  For a summer's day so long.

Till when their swords on their broad bucklers
    Were broken off in their hands,
'Hold your hand, hold your hand,' said Robin Hood,
    'And my merry men every one.

'For this is one of the best pinders
    That ever my eye did see,
But have you any meat,' said jolly Robin Hood,
    'For my merry men and me?'

'I have both bread and beef,' said the pinder,
    'And good ale of the best.'
'That is meat good enough,' said Robin Hood,
    'For any such unbidden guest.

'Oh, will you forsake your pinder's work,
    And live in the green wood with me?
You shall have a livery twice in the year,
    The one green, the other brown shall be.'

'At Michaelmas next my contract comes up,
    When every man gathers his fee;
Then I'll give as little for my master
    As he now gives for me.

'When Michaelmas day is come and gone,
    And my master has paid me my due,
Then I'll take my blue blade in my hand,
    And I'll come to the green wood with you.'

Robin Hood and
Allen a Dale

As Robin Hood in the forest stood,
    All under the greenwood tree,
There was he aware of a brave young man,
    As fine as fine might be.

The youngster was clad all in scarlet so red,
    In scarlet so red and fine,
A rose garland upon his head,
    And he chanted a happy rhyme.

As Robin Hood next morning stood,
    Amongst the leaves so green,
There did he see the same young man,
    Come drooping across the plain.

The garland he wore the day before,
    It was clean cast away,
And with every step he fetched a sigh,
    'Alack, and alas the day!'

Then stepped forth brave Little John,
    And Much, the miller's son,
Which made the young man bend his bow,
    As soon as he saw them come.

'Stand off, stand off!' the young man said,
    'What do you want with me?'
'You must come to see our master with me,
    Under the greenwood tree.'

And when he stood before bold Robin Hood,
   Robin asked him courteously,
'Oh, have you any money to spare
   For my merry men and me?'

'I have no money,' the young man said,
   'But five shillings and a ring,
And that I have kept for these seven long years,
   To have it at my wedding.

'I should yesterday have married a maid,
   But she is now from me ta'en,
To be the delight of a wealthy old knight,
   And so my poor heart is slain.'

'What is your name?' then said Robin Hood,
   'Come tell me, without any fail.'
'By the faith of my body,' then said the young man,
   'My name it is Allen a Dale.'

'What will you give me,' said bold Robin Hood,
   'In ready gold or gear,
To help you to win your true love again,
   And deliver her to you here?'

'I have no money,' then said the young man,
   'No ready gold nor fee,
But here I will swear upon all I hold dear
   Your own true servant to be.'

'Take off your fine clothing,' said bold Robin Hood,
   'And lay it upon a stone,
And put on another of Lincoln green
   To win your true love for your own.'

This young man soon did as Robin Hood bid—
  He cast off his clothing so fine,
And put on another of Lincoln green
  Just like all of Robin Hood's men.

Then Robin Hood hastened over the plain,
  And never once stopped he,
Till he came to the porch of that very church,
  Where the wedding was set to be.

'What brings you this way?' the priest he did say,
  'I'd have you now tell to me.'
'I am a fine harper,' then said Robin Hood,
  'The best in the north country.'

'Oh welcome, oh welcome,' the priest he did say,
  'That music best pleases me.'
'You shall have no music,' then said Robin Hood,
  'Till the bride and the bridegroom I see.'

With that there came in a wealthy knight,
  That was both grave and old,
And next to him was the daintiest lass,
  Who did shine like glistering gold.

'This is no fit match,' said bold Robin Hood,
  'That you do seem to make here,
And since Robin Hood has come into the church,
  The bride may choose her own dear.'

Then Robin Hood reached out to the bride,
  And he took her by the sleeve;
He led her before the church's door
  Without her father's leave.

'Tell me,' said he, 'and do not lie;
  The truth I'd have you say,
If ever you loved a man in your life
  That you should have married today.'

'Once I loved a bonny boy,
  I know that he loved me—
I'd rather beg for bread with him
  Than marry for gold and fee.'

'Would you know your love,' then said Robin Hood,
  'If you again him saw?'
'I'd know him again among three hundred men,
  If they were all here in a row.'

Then Robin Hood put his horn to his mouth,
  And he blew loud blasts three,
When four and twenty bowmen bold
  Came leaping over the lea.

And when they had come into the churchyard,
  Marching all in a row,
The first man of all was Allen a Dale,
  To give bold Robin his bow.

'This is your true love,' then said Robin Hood,
    'Young Allen, as I hear say,
And you shall be married at this same time,
    Before we depart away.'

There wasn't a one of the wedding guests
    That knew where to hide his head;
The priest slipped away among all that were there
    And into the bell house he fled.

'Come back, come back, you coward priest,
    It's not your place to flee,
When here is a bride and a bridegroom to wed,
    And I who will pay you their fee.'

Twenty shillings and a fine gold ring
    Robin Hood laid down on the book;
He told the priest to take what he thought fit,
    And the rest in the bride's glove he shook.

Then they brought forward the bride's father
    To give his consent by his hand:
'If you'll spare but my life, he may have as his wife
    My daughter and all of my land.'

Robin Hood and the
Bishop of Hereford

Some they will talk of lords and knights
    And some of barons bold,
But I'll tell you how Robin Hood served the bishop,
    When he robbed him of his gold.

As Robin he walked in merry Barnsdale
    Upon a morning in May,
Word came to him that the Bishop of Hereford
    Would come riding along that way.

'Come here, Little John,' said bold Robin Hood,
    'Come, kill me a good fat deer;
The Bishop of Hereford shall dine with me today,
    And he shall pay well for his cheer.'

'We'll kill a fat deer,' said bold Robin Hood,
    'And cook it by the highway side;
And we shall keep watch for the bishop in case
    By some other way he should ride.'

'You and I, master,' then said Little John,
    'We'll dress up in shepherd's attire,
And when the bishop comes riding along,
    We shall dance all about the fire.'

Robin Hood dressed himself in shepherd's attire
   With six of his yeomen also,
And when the Bishop of Hereford came by,
   All about the fire they did go.

'What do we have here?' then said the bishop,
   'And for whom do you make such a show?
Or why have you taken so much venison,
   When your company is so few?'

'We are poor shepherds,' said bold Robin Hood,
   'And we keep sheep all through the year,
But we are disposed to be merry this night
   And to feast on the king's fat deer.

'Will it please you to join us,' then said Robin Hood,
   'With all of your company,
And to eat your fill of a good fat buck,
   And to dine here in Barnsdale with me?'

'Nay, proud fellows!' the bishop said then,
   'But the king of your misdeeds shall know,
Therefore make haste and come along with me,
   For before the king you shall go.'

'Oh, pardon! Oh, pardon!' said bold Robin Hood,
   'Oh, pardon of you I pray!
For it does not befit a bishop's coat
   To take so many lives away.'

'No pardon, no pardon,' then said the bishop,
   'No pardon to you do I owe,
Therefore make haste and come along with me,
   For before the king you shall go.'

'Then I tell you, bishop,' said Robin Hood,
  'No longer can I forbear;
It's a pity that ever such a hard-hearted man
  A bishop's coat should wear!'

Then Robin set his back against a tree
  And his foot against a thorn,
And from underneath his shepherd's coat
  He pulled out a bugle horn.

He put that horn up to his mouth
  And a loud blast he did blow,
Till threescore and ten of bold Robin Hood's men
  Came running all in a row.

They all made a reverence to bold Robin Hood,
  And a comely sight it was to see.
'What is the matter, master,' they said,
  'That you blow so hastily?'

'Oh, here is the Bishop of Hereford,
  And he will not show charity to me,
And he will not come to dine along with us
  Under the greenwood tree.

'But he says we must all go along with him
  And before the king we must go,
And when we come before our royal king,
  Our misdeeds he means to show.

'And the king he has made an outlaw of me
  And of you good yeomen also,
And if ever we come before our royal king,
  Our lives will be lost, as I know.

'But as for the Bishop of Hereford,
　No pardon from him can we crave.'
'Then cut off his head, master,' said Little John,
　'And throw him into his grave.'

'Oh, pardon! Oh, pardon!' the bishop then said,
　'Oh, pardon of you I pray!
For if I had known that it had been you,
　I'd have gone by some other way.'

'No pardon, no pardon,' said Robin Hood,
　'No pardon to you do I owe;
Therefore make haste and come along with me
　For to merry Barnsdale you shall go.'

Then Robin Hood took the bishop by the hand
　And led him to merry Barnsdale,
And he made him to stay and sup with him that night
　And to drink wine, beer and ale.

'Eat up your dinner,' said Robin Hood,
　'As it is to be your lot.
I may pardon your life, proud bishop,' he said,
　'But your purse I may pardon not!'

'Call in the reckoning,' said the bishop,
　'For I guess it must be very dear.'
'Lend me your purse, bishop,' said Little John,
　'And I'll see that you pay for your cheer.'

Then Little John took his shepherd's coat,
    And spread it out on the ground,
And straightaway from the bishop's bags
    He counted three hundred pound.

'Here's money enough, master,' said Little John,
    'And a comely sight it is to see,
And I have some charity for the bishop now,
    Though I know he has none for me.'

'Set that to one side, John,' said Robin Hood,
    'For before the bishop may pass,
And before he may get out of Barnsdale again,
    I would hear him sing me a Mass.'

'Oh, pardon me, yeoman,' the bishop then said,
    'Oh, pardon me I pray!
But it is too late now to sing a Mass,
    For it's past three o'clock in the day.'

'You may sing me a Mass,' said bold Robin Hood,
    'For all your haste and speed,
As I do not think it can ever be too late
    To do such a holy deed.'

Then Robin Hood took the bishop by the hand,
    And tied him tight to a tree,
And he made him sing a Mass, by God,
    To bless all his yeomanry.

'Come now, proud bishop,' said Robin Hood,
  'Though you feel no charity to me,
We will dance around and be merry of heart,
  Round about the greenwood tree.'

Robin Hood took the bishop by the hand,
  And he caused the music to play,
And he made the bishop to dance in his boots,
  Before he could get away.

'Kneel down now, bishop,' said Robin Hood,
  'Before from us you depart,
And swear that for all we have done to you here,
  You forgive us with all your heart.'

'God's curse upon me,' the bishop said then,
  'If I do not say what is true,
And for all that you ever have done to me,
  I freely forgive it of you.'

Then Robin Hood took the bishop by the hand,
  And set him on his way again,
And then he shared out all the bishop's gold
  In Barnsdale with his merry men.

Robin Hood and the Potter

I

In summer, when the blossoms bloom,
  And the leaves grow on every tree,
The small birds sing in the merry green wood
  As merrily as can be.

Listen now, good yeomen,
  Comely, courteous, and good,
One of the best that ever bore bow,
  His name was Robin Hood.

Robin Hood was the yeoman's name,
  So courteous, as I hear;
For the love of Our Lady,
  All women he did revere.

As this good yeoman stood one day,
  Among his merry band,
There he was aware of a proud potter,
  Came driving over the land.

'See where there comes a proud potter,' said Robin,
  'That often has come this way,
But he was never so courteous a man
  One penny in passage to pay.'

'I met him at Wentbridge,' said Little John,
   'So ill may him betide!
For three such strokes he gave to me
   As nearly split my side.

'I'll wager forty shillings,' said Little John,
   'And I'll pay it here today,
There's not a man among us all
   Could make him passage pay.'

'Then here is forty shillings,' said Robin,
   'And more, if you'll agree,
That I shall make that proud potter,
   Pay his passage to me.'

This money that they laid there,
   They put in a yeoman's hand;
Then Robin rushed up to the potter,
   And ordered him to stand.

He put his hand upon his horse,
   And ordered him to stand;
The potter quickly said to him,
   'Mate, what do you want?'

'For three years and more now, potter,' he said,
   'You've often come this way,
And yet you've never been courteous enough
   One penny in passage to pay.'

'What is your name,' the potter said,
   'That you ask for passage from me?'
'Robin Hood it is my name,
   And you'll give me your fee.'

'I'll give no fee,' the potter said,
   'Nor passage will I pay;
Now, get your hands from off my horse,
   Or else you'll rue the day!'

This potter leapt down from his horse
   And to his cart he strode,
He took a good two-handed staff,
   And turned on Robin Hood.

Robin had a buckler at his side
   His good sword there he drew;
The potter said to Robin Hood,
   'Mate, let my horse go!'

These two yeomen then came to blows,
   It was a good sight to see,
And Robin's men they laughed at it,
   As they stood under a tree.

Little John said to his fellows there,
   'That potter will staunchly stand.'
The potter, with a backhand blow,
   Struck the buckler from Robin's hand.

And as Robin stooped to pick it up
    Where it had fallen down,
The potter got him on the neck,
    And knocked him to the ground.

Robin's men were looking on,
    As they stood under a bough;
'Let's help our master,' said Little John,
    'Or else he'll kill him now.'

Then did these yeomen in great haste,
    Up to their master run.
Said Little John to his master,
    'Who has the wager won?

'Shall I have your forty shillings,' said Little John,
    'Or master, shall you have mine?'
'If it was a hundred shillings,' said Robin,
    'It would all be yours this time.'

'It's hardly courteous,' said the potter,
    'As I've heard wise men say,
When a poor yeoman comes driving along the road,
    To stop him on his way.'

'Indeed, it's true,' said Robin Hood,
    'You speak good Yeomanry,
And if you drive along here every day,
    You'll never be stopped by me.'

'Good potter, may I ask,' said Robin,
    'This fellowship of you?
Give me your clothing, and you'll have mine,
    And I'll to Nottingham go.'

'I'll do that,' said the potter,
　'Your fellow I'll remain,
And if you cannot sell my pots,
　Bring them back here again.'

'Not so indeed,' said Robin,
　'A curse upon my head,
If I bring any pots back here again,
　That I could have sold instead.'

Then out spoke Little John,
　And all the merry men,
'Beware the Sheriff of Nottingham, master,
　For he is not our friend.'

'With the blessing of Our Lady,
　I will come safely through.
Giddy up! Walk on!' said Robin,
　'To Nottingham I'll go.'

Robin went to Nottingham,
　Those pots for to sell;
The potter stayed with Robin's men,
　Where he need fear no ill.

Then Robin drove upon his way,
　So merrily over the land.
There's more to tell that's yet to say,
　The best is now at hand.

II

When Robin came to Nottingham,
   Indeed as I do say,
He quickly tethered up his horse,
   And gave it oats and hay.

It was in the middle of the town,
   Where he set out his store;
'Pots! pots!' he cried aloud,
   'Free gifts if you buy more!'

It was right outside the sheriff's gate
   That he his trade did ply;
Wives and widows gathered round,
   And soon began to buy.

'Pots, cheap pots!' cried Robin still,
   'I don't want any left.'
And everyone that saw him sell
   Said he didn't know his craft.

He sold the pots for three pence,
   That should have sold for five,
And man and wife said privately,
   'That potter can never thrive.'

Robin sold his pots so fast,
   That soon he had just five;
He took the last pots off his cart,
   To send to the sheriff's wife.

She was delighted with his gift,
   'I thank you, sir,' she said,
And when you next come back this way,
   I'll buy your pots, indeed.'

'You shall have the best,' said Robin,
   'I swear by the Trinity.'
Most courteously she said to him,
   'Come, dine with the sheriff and me.'

'I thank you, my lady,' said Robin,
   'Your bidding I will do.'
A serving girl took the pots inside,
   And Robin followed too.

When Robin came into the hall
   The sheriff there to meet,
The potter knew his courtesy,
   And did the sheriff greet.

'Look, sir, what this potter has given us,
   Five pots, both small and great!'
'He is most welcome,' said the sheriff,
   'Let's wash, and go to eat.'

As they sat down to take their meal,
  With noble cheer likewise,
Two of the sheriff's men spoke there
  About a worthy prize.

A shooting match both fair and fine
  Was shortly to begin,
With forty shillings prize money
  For whoever should win.

In silence sat this proud potter,
  And to himself thought he,
As I am a true Christian man,
  This shooting will I see.

When they had eaten of the best,
  With bread and ale and wine,
To the targets they went in haste,
  With bows and arrows fine.

The sheriff's men were archers good,
  They shot with all their strength,
But none of them came near the mark
  By half a good bow length.

In silence stood the proud potter;
  Then aloud said he,
'If I had a bow now, by the Lord,
  A good shot you should see.'

'You shall have a bow,' said the sheriff,
  'From three you may choose the best;
As you seem a strong and sturdy fellow,
  We'll put you to the test.'

The sheriff commanded a yeoman there
  A choice of bows to bring;
On the best bow that the yeoman brought
  Robin set a string.

'Now we'll know if you're any good,
  If you pull it up to your ear.'
'So help me God,' said the proud potter,
  'But this is very weak gear.'

Then to the quiver Robin went,
  And a good arrow he took;
So near the mark did Robin shoot,
  It came within a foot.

All of them shot about again,
  The sheriff's men and he;
He did not fail to hit his mark,
  He split the stave in three.

The sheriff's men felt great shame
  This potter should have won;
The sheriff laughed and made light of it,
  Saying, 'Potter, you're the man.

'You are the man,' the sheriff said,
　'And worthy to bear a bow
Take this good bow here with you now
　Wherever you may go.'

'In my cart I have a bow,
　One that indeed is good;
In my cart there is the bow
　I got from Robin Hood.'

'Do you know Robin Hood?' said the sheriff,
　'Potter, do please tell me.'
'A hundred turns I have shot with him,
　Under his trestle tree.'

The sheriff swore a mighty oath,
　He swore by the Trinity,
'I had rather than a hundred pounds
　That false outlaw stood before me.'

'If you will do as I do say,' said the potter,
　'And boldly go with me,
Then in the morning, before we eat bread,
　Robin Hood we shall see.'

'I will reward you,' said the sheriff,
　And he swore by God so great.
They finished shooting, and home they went,
　Where supper was already set.

III

Early next morning, when it was day,
   He readied himself to ride;
The potter began to hitch up his cart,
   And would not leave it behind.

He took his leave of the sheriff's wife,
   And thanked her for everything:
'If you'll wear it, my lady, for my love,
   Let me give you this gold ring.'

'I thank you, sir,' said the sheriff's wife,
   'May God your guardian be.'
The sheriff's heart was never so keen
   The fair forest to see.

And when they came to the fair forest,
   Under the leaves of green,
The birds sang out on every bough,
   It was a great joy to be seen.

'Here it is merry to be,' said Robin,
   'For a man that has money to spend,
And by my horn we soon shall find
   If Robin is here at hand.'

Robin put his horn to his mouth,
  And blew a blast full good,
That was heard by all his merry men
  Where under the trees they stood.

It was heard by all his merry men
  Deep down within the wood.
'I hear my master blow,' said Little John,
  And they ran as if they were mad.

And when they came to their master,
  Out called Little John;
'Master, how did you do in Nottingham?
  And are your pots all gone?'

'Aye, by goodness, Little John,
  Look you, have no fear;
I have brought the Sheriff of Nottingham,
  For all our business here.'

'He is most welcome,' said Little John,
  'This news is very good.'
The sheriff had rather than a hundred pounds
  He had never seen Robin Hood.

'Had I known then what now I know,
  In Nottingham when we were,
You should not have come to the fair forest
  In all this thousand year.'

'I know that well,' said Robin,
  'And thank God that you are here,
So now, you must leave your horse with us,
  And all your other gear.'

'Oh, God forbid,' the sheriff said,
  That I should so lose my goods,
That I, the Sheriff of Nottingham,
  Should be tricked by Robin Hood.'

'You came here on your horse so high,
  And home you'll go on foot,
But greet your wife when you get home,
  That woman is so good.

'I shall send to her a white palfrey,
  That ambles in its gait;
Were it not for the love of your sweet wife,
  More sorrow would you await.'

Thus parted Robin Hood and the sheriff,
  Who to Nottingham made his way;
His loving wife welcomed him back home,
  And to him she did say,

'Sir, how did you do in the green forest?
  And have you brought Robin home?'
'The devil take him, both body and bone;
  I have suffered dreadful scorn.

'He took everything that I brought to the wood,
  My goods and my gear too,
All but this fine palfrey,
  That he has sent to you.'

At that she started to laugh aloud,
  And swore by the Trinity,
'Now you have paid for all the pots
  That Robin gave to me!

'Now you are home in Nottingham.
  You shall have gear and goods.'
But we must tell of Robin Hood,
  And the potter in the green woods.

'Potter, what were your pots worth
  That I took to Nottingham?'
'Ten shillings is what I reckon
  I could have got for them.'

'You shall have ten pounds,' said Robin,
  'Of money fair and free,
And whenever you come to the green wood,
  You're welcome, potter, to me.'

Thus parted Robin, the sheriff, and the potter,
  Under the greenwood tree;
God have mercy on Robin Hood's soul,
  And save all good yeomanry!

Robin Hood and
the Monk

In summer, when the woods are bright,
   And leaves are large and long,
It is full merry in the fair forest
   To hear the birds in song,

To see the deer draw to the dale,
   And leave the hills so steep,
And shelter among the leaves of green,
   Within the green wood deep.

It happened on a Whitsuntide
   Early one May morning,
The sun above began to shine,
   And the birds to merrily sing.

'It's a merry morning,' said Little John,
   'By Him that died on tree;
There's no merrier man than I am now
   In all Christianity.

'Pluck up your heart, my dear master,'
   Little John did say,
'And think how it is a full fair time
   Upon a morning in May.'

'One thing still grieves me,' said Robin,
  'And brings my heart much woe;
That I may not on such a solemn day
  To Mass nor Matins go.

'It is a fortnight and more,' said he,
  'Since my Saviour I did see;
Today I'll go to Nottingham,' said Robin,
  'By the might of mild Mary.'

Then up spoke Much, the miller's son—
  May good luck him betide!
'Take twelve of your brave yeomen, Robin,
  Well weaponed, at your side,

'Let each man bear his bow with him,
  And a good sword at his side,
For someone who might kill you alone,
  Dare not all twelve abide.'

'Of all my merry men,' said Robin,
  'I will take none with me,
But Little John shall bear my bow,
  And keep me company.'

'You can bear your bow yourself, master,
  'And I'll take mine with me,
And we'll shoot for a penny,' said Little John,
  'Under the greenwood tree.'

'I'll not shoot for a penny,' said Robin Hood,
  'Though you may shoot with me,
But for every penny of yours,' said Robin,
  'I will wager three.'

So they went shooting, these yeomen two,
    Both at bush and broom,
Till Little John from his master
    Five shillings he has won.

An awful row between them rose,
    As they went on their way;
Little John said he'd won five shillings,
    And Robin Hood said crossly, 'Nay!'

Robin Hood struck Little John,
    And said that he had lied;
Then Little John drew the shining sword,
    That hung down by his side.

'If you weren't my master,' said Little John,
    'You'd pay for this full sore;
Go get yourself another man,
    For I'll serve you no more.'

Then Robin went to Nottingham
    By himself, forlorn, alone,
And Little John went to merry Sherwood,
    Where the paths he knew each one.

When Robin got to Nottingham,
    As I may tell you plain,
He prayed to God and Mary mild
    To bring him safe out again.

He went into St Mary's church,
    And kneeled before the cross;
There everyone inside the church
    Could see where Robin was.

Beside him stood a fat-headed monk,
  I pray God bring him woe!
He saw it was good Robin Hood,
  And quickly did him know.

Out at the church door he went,
  As fast as he could run,
And all the gates of Nottingham
  He had them barred each one.

'Rise up,' he said, 'you proud sheriff,
  Get ready with good speed,
For I have spied the king's felon,
  He's in this town indeed.

'I have spied the false felon,
  As he stood at Mass this day;
You'll be to blame,' then said the monk,
  'If you let him get away.

'This traitor's name is Robin Hood,
  Under the greenwood tree;
He robbed me once of a hundred pounds—
  It's still a grief to me.'

Up then rose this proud sheriff,
  And swiftly he set out,
And he has gone to St Mary's Church
  With his men all about.

In at the doors they boldly pressed,
  With staves full many a one;
'Alas, alas!' said Robin Hood,
  'Now, I miss Little John.'

But Robin pulled out a two-hand sword,
  That hung down by his knee,
And wherever the sheriff's men stood thickest,
  That's where Robin would be.

Three times he ran among them all,
  Indeed as I do say;
He wounded many a mother's son,
  And twelve he killed that day.

But upon the helm on the sheriff's head
  He broke his sword in two;
'A curse upon the smith,' said Robin,
  'That ever he made you!

'For now I am left weaponless,
  Alas, against my will,
And unless I can flee from these traitors,
  I know they will me kill.'

Robin went among them all,
  And into the church he ran,
But none would give him sanctuary,
  And they seized that good yeoman.

And they have sent that fat-headed monk
  That he the king should tell,
But Robin got word to his merry men
  To say what there befell.

Some fell down faint as if they were dead,
  And lay as still as stone;
Not one among them kept his head
  Except for Little John.

'Give up your grief,' said Little John,
  'For Him that died on tree!
In you that should be valiant men,
  It's a shameful sight to see.

'Our master has been hard beset
  But still can get away;
Pluck up your hearts, and leave your moans,
  And listen to what I say:

'He has served Our Lady for many a day,
  And does so still indeed,
So I trust in her especially
  To help him in his need.

'Therefore be glad,' said Little John,
  'And leave this mourning be,
For I shall be this monk's guide,
  With the help of mild Mary.

'I'll take my good bow in my hand
  As I go along the way,
And none but Much, the miller's son,
  Shall bear me company.

'The monk has gone with his own page
  To tell the king, I know,
But if I can catch him,' said Little John,
  'We two instead shall go.

'Be sure to maintain our trestle tree,
  Under the leaves so small,
And eat well of the fallow deer,
  That go about the dale.'

Then Little John and Much set forth,
   Together as I say,
And stopped at Much's uncle's house
   That stood by the highway.

Little John looked out of a high window,
   To see what he could spy,
And he saw the monk and his little page boy,
   As they came riding by.

'By my faith,' said Little John to Much,
   'I can tell you news that's good—
I see where the monk comes riding;
   I know him by his wide hood.'

These two yeomen went off to the road,
   As they did so intend;
They asked what news the monk might know,
   As if they'd been his friend.

'Where have you come from?' said Little John,
   'Come tell what news you may,
For I heard that false outlaw, Robin Hood,
   Was taken yesterday.

'He robbed me and both my friends
   Of everything we had;
If that false outlaw has been caught,
   Indeed we would be glad.'

'He robbed me too,' said the monk,
   Of a hundred pounds and more;
But I was first to set hands on him—
   You may thank me therefore.'

'May God thank you,' said Little John,
   'And we will when we may;
We'll travel with you, if you like,
   And help you on your way,

'For Robin Hood has many wild fellows,
   That live throughout this wood,
And if they knew you rode this way,
   They'd kill you if they could.'

As they went talking along the way,
   This monk and Little John,
John took the monk's horse by the rein,
   And so he led him on.

John took the monk's horse by the rein,
   Indeed as I do say,
And so did Much with the little page,
   So he could not get away.

John grabbed the bottom of his hood
   And pulled the monk right down;
He took so little care of him,
   The monk's head hit the ground.

Little John was so enraged,
   The monk knew he would die,
And when he saw him draw his sword,
   Loud mercy he did cry.

'He was my master,' said Little John,
   'That you have cast in jail,
But you'll never get to meet our king,
   Or tell to him your tale.'

John struck off the monk's head,
   And quickly did him kill,
And so did Much with the little page,
   For fear that he would tell.

They buried them there upon the moor,
   Among the heather and ling,
And together Little John and Much
   Took the letters to our king.

When Little John came before the king
   He kneeled down on the ground;
'God save you, my liege lord,' he said,
   'And keep you safe and sound!

'God save you, my liege king!' he said.
   To speak John was full bold;
He put the letters into the king's hand,
   And the king did them unfold.

And when our king those letters read,
   'Upon my life!' said he,
'There was never a yeoman in merry England
   That I longed more to see.

'Where's the monk that should have brought these letters?'
   Our king he then did say.
'To tell the truth,' said Little John,
   'He died along the way.'

The king gave Much and Little John
   Twenty pounds and ten,
And made them yeomen of the crown,
   And bade them set off again.

He put his own seal into Little John's hand,
  That he to the sheriff should bring,
To show he'd been sent for Robin Hood,
  To take him to the king.

John took his leave of our king,
  In truth as I do say;
By the shortest road to Nottingham
  He quickly made his way.

And when John came to Nottingham
  He found the gates were locked;
John called up to the gatekeeper,
  To have the way unblocked.

'What is the cause,' said Little John,
  'You bar the gates so fast?'
'Because of Robin Hood,' he said,
  'In prison deep he's cast.

'John and Much and Will Scarlock,
  Indeed as I do say,
They kill our men upon our walls,
  And attack us every day.'

Little John asked for the sheriff,
  And soon he has him found;
Then he took out the king's own seal,
  And put it into his hand.

When the sheriff saw the king's seal,
  He doffed the hood from his head;
'Where is the monk that took the letters?'
  To Little John he said.

'The king's so pleased with him,' said John,
    'Indeed as I do say,
He has made him Abbot of Westminster,
    The lord of that abbey.'

The sheriff feasted Little John,
    And gave him wine of the best;
At night they all went to their beds,
    And every man to his rest.

But when the sheriff was asleep,
    Drunk from wine and ale,
Little John and Much together
    Made their way to the jail.

Little John called for the jailer,
    And told him to get up soon;
He said Robin Hood had broken out,
    And from prison he was gone.

The jailer got up as quick as he could,
    As soon as he heard John call;
Little John was ready with a sword,
    And stabbed him through to the wall.

'Now I'll be jailer,' said Little John,
    And took the keys in his hand;
He made his way to Robin Hood,
    And soon had him unbound.

He gave him a good sword in his hand,
    His head therewith to keep,
And there where the city walls were lowest
    They lightly down did leap.

But when the cock began to crow,
    And day had just begun,
The sheriff found the jailer dead,
    And the common bell was rung.

He put the word about the town,
    That, be he yeoman or knave,
Whoever could bring him Robin Hood,
    A good reward should have.

'For I dare never,' said the sheriff,
    'Come before our king,
For if I do, I know for sure
    Indeed he will me hang.'

The sheriff searched through Nottingham,
    As thoroughly as could be,
But Robin was in merry Sherwood,
    As light as leaf on tree.

Then up spoke good Little John,
    To Robin Hood he did say,
'I've done you a good turn for a bad;
    Repay me when you may.

'I've done you a good turn,' said John,
    'Indeed as I do say;
I have brought you under the greenwood tree,
    So farewell, and have a good day.'

'Nay, by my faith,' said Robin,
   'For that shall never be;
I make you master,' said Robin Hood,
   'Of all my men and me.'

'Nay, by my faith,' said Little John,
   'For that shall never be,
But let me be your man,' said John,
   'And that will best please me.'

So John got Robin Hood out of jail,
   Indeed as I have said;
When his men saw him safe and sound,
   They were content and glad.

They poured the wine and made merry,
   Under the leaves so small,
And ate pasties of venison,
   That tasted good with ale.

Then word came to our comely king
   How Robin Hood was gone,
And how the sheriff of Nottingham
   Dared not him look upon.

Then out spoke our comely king,
   An angry man was he:
'If Little John has deceived the sheriff,
   In faith, so has he me.

'Little John has deceived us both,
    And that full well I see,
Or else the Sheriff of Nottingham
    Should be hanged from a tree.

'I made them yeomen of the crown,
    And gave them money in hand;
I gave them pardon,' said our king,
    'Throughout all merry England.

'I gave them pardon,' said our king,
    'Upon the life of me,
And of all the yeomen in merry England,
    There's none so good as he.

'He's true to his master,' said our king,
    'By sweet St John most blessed,
And he has more love for Robin Hood
    Than he has for all the rest.

'Robin Hood is forever bound to him,
    Whether in street or stall;
Speak no more of the matter,' said our king,
    'But John has deceived us all.'

Thus ends the talking of the monk
    And of Robin Hood;
May God, that is crowned King of Kings,
    Bring us all to good!

Robin Hood and
the three Squires

There are twelve months in every year,
    As I hear people say,
But the merriest month in all the year
    Is the merry month of May.

As Robin was ranging the forest all round,
    With a-link, a-down and a-day,
It was there he met with a poor old woman,
    Came weeping along the highway.

'Why are you weeping?' bold Robin he said,
    'Come tell the cause to me.'
'Oh! I do weep for my three sons,
    For they're all condemned to die.'

'What church have they robbed?' said bold Robin Hood,
    'Or what parish priest have they slain?
Or have they forced maidens against their will?
    Or with other men's wives have lain?'

'No church have they robbed, good sir,' she said,
    'No parish priest have they slain;
No maids have they forced against their will,
    Nor with other men's wives have they lain.'

'Oh, what have they done then?' said bold Robin Hood,
   'Come tell me full speedily.'
'It is for slaying the king's fallow deer,
   That they're all condemned to die.'

'Then go home, go home,' said bold Robin Hood,
   'Go home full speedily,
And I will go to fair Nottingham town,
   For the sake of the squires all three.'

Now Robin Hood is to Nottingham gone,
   To Nottingham straightaway,
And there he met with a poor beggar man,
   Came creeping along the highway.

'What news? what news, my poor old man?
   Come, tell what news you may.'
'There is weeping and wailing in fair Nottingham,
   For the death of three squires this day.'

'Come change your clothes with me, old man.
   In faith, you shall have mine,
And here's forty shillings in good silver,
   To spend on ale or wine.'

'Your clothes are of good Lincoln green,
   But mine are ragged and torn,
And it is unseemly and unkind,
   To laugh an old man to scorn.'

'I mean no scorn, old man,' says Robin,
   'Come change your clothes with mine,
And here's twenty pieces of good broad gold,
   To feast your friends with wine.'

Then Robin put on the old man's hood,
　　It wobbled upon his crown;
'When I come into Nottingham,' said Robin Hood,
　　'My hood will come lightly down.'

Then Robin put on the old man's cloak,
　　It was torn about the neck;
'Now, by my faith,' said Will Scarlock,
　　'Fine clothes the man do make.'

Then Robin put on the old man's breeches,
　　They were torn all up the side;
'Now, by my faith,' said Little John,
　　'This man loved little pride.'

Then Robin put on the old man's hose,
　　They were torn about the knee;
'When I look at my legs,' said bold Robin Hood,
　　'I could laugh for what I see.'

Now Robin Hood is to Nottingham gone,
　　With a-link, a-down and a-down,
And there he met with the proud sheriff,
　　Came walking through the town.

'A boon, a boon, great master sheriff,
　　One boon I beg on my knee,
And what will you give to a poor old man
　　That today would your hangman be?'

'If for the deaths of these three squires,
　　Their hangman you would be,
Then you shall have all their fine clothing,
　　And all their silver money.'

'Oh, I will have none of their fine clothing,
  Nor none of their silver money,
But I'll have three blasts on my bugle horn,
  That their souls into heaven may flee.

'I have a horn in my bag,' he said.
  'I got it from Robin Hood,
And so when I set my horn to my mouth,
  For you it will blow little good.'

'Then blow your horn, blow your horn!' said the sheriff,
  'Of your blasts I have no doubt,
And I hope that you blow on your horn so hard,
  That both your eyes fall out.'

Then Robin Hood turned him round about,
  And jumped over stock and stone,
And everyone that saw Robin Hood run,
  Said he was a nimble old man.

Then Robin Hood mounted the gallows so high,
  And a loud blast he did blow,
Till a hundred and ten of bold Robin Hood's men
  Came running all in a row.

'Now, bend your bows and stretch your bowstrings,
  Set the gallows tree all about,
And a curse on his heart,' said bold Robin Hood,
  'That would let the proud sheriff get out.'

When the sheriff did see gentle Robin would shoot,
    He held up both his hands.
Says, 'Ask, good Robin, and you shall have,
    Whether it be houses or lands.'

'I will neither have houses nor lands,' said Robin,
    'Nor gold, nor none of your fee,
But I will have those squires all three
    To come to the green wood with me.'

'But God forbid,' then said the proud sheriff,
    'That ever that should be,
For these men are the king's felons,
    And so are condemned to die.'

'I was never a hangman in all my life,
    Nor ever will be to my trade,
And a curse on his heart,' said bold Robin Hood,
    'That first was hangman made.

'But grant me my asking,' said bold Robin Hood,
    'Or by the faith of my body,
You shall yourself be the very first man
    To hang on this gallows tree.'

'Then take them, then take them,' said the sheriff,
    'Then take them along with you,
For there's never a man in all Nottingham
    That can do the like of you.'

Robin Hood and the Old Woman

Between a crag and a stony rock,
   Upon a summer's day,
Over a pleasant running brook
   Robin Hood took his way.

It was about the midsummer time,
   And he was a weary chap,
And there upon a pleasant bank
   He lay down to take a nap.

But by the thunder of horse's hooves
   He was woken up again,
And he saw where the sheriff and all of his men
   Came riding over the plain.

Away then ran good Robin Hood,
   For he dared no longer bide,
Until he saw a little house
   Down by the river side.

And when he came to this little house,
   He found an old woman within,
And she was sitting down by the fireside,
   Where she did sit and spin.

'Oh, help me! Oh, help me, my good old woman!
   For God's love, please help me!
For here comes the Sheriff with all of his men,
   And I fear they are after me.'

'Why, who are you,' the old woman said,
   'That you think I can do you some good?'
'I am an outlaw, my lady,' he said,
   'And they call me Robin Hood.'

'If you're Robin Hood,' the old woman said,
   'Then I'll keep you from your foes,
For you gave me twelve pence once on a time,
   To buy me stockings and shoes.

It was against the frost and snow,
   As I never shall forget,
But before you leave my house again,
   I will repay the debt.

So lend to me your fancy clothes,
   And you can put on mine;
Here, have my veil and my russet gown,
   And take up my spindle and twine.

And string for me your noble bow,
   For it is too strong for me,
And at the sheriff I'll pretend to shoot
   And all his company.'

With that the sheriff came to the door,
   And he called in a furious mood,
'Now yield, now yield, you bold outlaw,
   You traitor, Robin Hood!'

'I will not yield,' the old woman said,
   'You shall not yet take me,
For here under my girdle I have
   Thirty good arrows and three.

For here under my girdle I have
    Thirty good arrows I know,
And every arrow may kill a man,
    And one of them may kill you.'

'If you'll give up your bow,' the sheriff said,
    'And give up your body to me,
Then I will carry you safe and sound,
    And take you to King Henry.'

The old woman he set on a milk white steed,
    Himself on a dapple grey,
And for joy that he'd taken Robin Hood,
    He rode singing along the highway.

But Robin has gone to the good green wood
    As fast as he could go,
With the old woman's veil and russet gown,
    Her spindle and twine also.

'Who's that? Who's that,' said Will Scarlock,
    'That's coming over the ditch?
A broad arrow I'll let fly at her,
    She looks just like a witch.'

'Oh, hold your hand,' said Robin then,
    'Don't shoot your arrows so keen,
For I am your master, Robin Hood,
    As quickly shall be seen.'

Then Robin Hood threw off his veil,
    Which he had been wrapped in,
And then they knew their dear master
    By the beard upon his chin.

The sheriff rode singing along the highway,
    Most comely to be seen,
Till he saw a hundred brave bowmen bold,
    All dressed in Lincoln green.

'Oh, who is that,' the sheriff said,
    'That's ranging down in the wood?'
'If I'm not mistaken,' the old woman said,
    'I think it is Robin Hood.'

'Then who are you?' the sheriff said,
    'That I have here with me?'
'I am an old woman,' the old woman said,
    'Lift up my leg and see!'

'Then, woe is me,' the sheriff said,
    'That ever I saw this day.'
He turned around and away he rode,
    For he dared no longer stay.

Then Robin took off the old woman's gown,
    And he threw it down on the ground,
He took the milk white steed from her,
    And he gave her twenty pound.

Robin Hood and
Guy of Gisburn

Robin he walks in the green forest,
   As blithe as a bird in a tree,
But he that fetches good Robin's head,
   He'll win both knights and fee.

Sir Guy has gone to Nottingham
   And there he made a vow,
'I'll take the head of Robin Hood,
   And I'll bring it here to you.'

'You're a good man,' said the proud sheriff,
   'And I'll give you knights and fee,
If you take the head of Robin Hood
   And you bring it here to me.'

But Robin he walks in the green forest,
   Under his trestle tree,
Says, 'Listen, listen, my merry men,
   What news is come to me.

'The sheriff he has given word
   That he would have my head,
But before this twelvemonth comes to an end,
   I may have his instead.

'Look to yourselves, my merry men,
   For John shall come with me.'
And we'll go and find this false yeoman,
   Wherever he may be.'

They've put on their gowns of green,
    And shooting gone are they,
Until they came to the merry green wood,
    Where they loved best to be.

And when they came to the merry green wood,
    Where they loved best to be,
There were they aware of a big yeoman,
    With his back against a tree.

A sword and dagger he wore at his side,
    That many a man had slain,
And he was dressed in his horse's hide,
    Top and tail and mane.

'Stay here, master,' said Little John,
    'Under this trestle tree,
And I will go to this big yeoman
    To see what I can see.'

'Ah, John, you set no store by me!
    Now, tell if you can find
That ever I sent my men before,
    And tarried myself behind.

'It isn't hard to spot a fool,
    When you've heard what he has said;
If it weren't for the breaking of my bow,
    Now, John, I'd break your head!'

But unkind words bring little love,
    That parted Robin and John,
And John set out for Barnsdale,
    Where the paths he knows each one.

And when he came to Barnsdale,
   Great sorrow there he had,
For he found two of his own fellows
   Were slain both in a glade.

Will Scarlock was fleeing fast afoot
   Over both stock and stone,
And the sheriff with seven score of his men
   Fast after him has gone.

'One shot I'll shoot,' says Little John.
   'I swear by almighty God,
I'll make my friend who flees so fast
   To be both merry and glad.'

John has bent his good long bow
   And readied himself to shoot,
But the bow was made of a tender bough
   And fell broken at his foot.

'My curse upon the bow,' said John,
   'That ever it grew on tree,
For when it should have been a blessing,
   It has been a curse to me.'

This shot it was but loosely shot,
   The arrow flew in vain,
And it hit one of the sheriff's men;
   Good William a Trent was slain.

It had been better for William a Trent
   To hang upon the gallow,
Than for him to lie in the green wood there,
   Slain with an arrow.

As it is said, when men are met,
  Six can do more than three,
So have they taken Little John,
  And tied him tight to a tree.

'You'll be dragged over dale and down,' said the sheriff,
  'And hanged high upon a hill.'
'You may yet fail,' said Little John,
  'If it be Christ's own will.'

Let us leave talking of Little John,
  As he is tied tight to a tree,
And talk of Guy and Robin Hood
  In the green wood where they be.

'I'm after an outlaw,' said Sir Guy,
  'Men call him Robin Hood;
I'd rather meet with him today
  Than forty pounds of gold.'

'If you two met, you soon would see
  Which one of you was better,
But let's make some other pastime here,
  As we walk in the woods together.

'Let's make some other pastime here,
  Or other pastime find,
And perhaps we'll meet with Robin Hood
  At some unlooked for time.'

So, they cut down the summer boughs
  That grew below the briar,
And set them up at a hundred yards,
  To shoot the staves full near.

The first shot that good Robin shot,
   Struck right beside the bough;
Guy was an archer good enough,
   But he could never shoot so.

The second shot Sir Guy did shoot,
   He shot the garland through,
But Robin Hood shot better yet;
   He split the mark in two.

'God's blessing on your heart!' says Guy.
   'Good fellow, your shooting is good,
And if your heart is as good as your hands,
   You're better than Robin Hood.

'Tell me your name, good fellow,' says Guy,
   'Among the greenwood flowers.'
'Nay, by my faith,' said good Robin,
   'Till you have told me yours.'

'I've lived by dale and down,' said Guy,
   'And done many a wicked turn,
And he that calls me by my right name
   Calls me Guy of good Gisburn.'

'My home is in the wood,' says Robin,
   'Of you I think right nought;
My name's Robin Hood of Barnsdale,
   A fellow you have long sought.'

He who had neither been kith nor kin
   Might have seen a full fair sight,
As these two yeomen set to together
   With sword blades flashing bright.

To have seen how these yeomen fought,
    For two hours on a summer's day,
And neither Guy nor Robin Hood
    Once tried to run away.

But Robin stumbled over a root,
    And fell upon the ground,
And Guy was quick and nimble of foot
    And struck when he was down.

'Ah, dear Lady!' said Robin Hood,
    'You are both Mother and Maid!
I think it was never a man's destiny
    To die before his day.

Robin thought on Our Lady dear,
    And soon leapt up again,
And when he struck with a backhand blow,
    Sir Guy of Gisburn was slain.

He took Sir Guy's head by the hair,
    And stuck it on his bow's end:
'You have been a traitor all your life,
    And that must have an end.'

Robin pulled out an Irish knife
    And cut Sir Guy in the face,
So none who was ever of woman born
    Could tell who Sir Guy was.

Says, 'Lie there, lie there now, Sir Guy,
    And with me be not wroth;
If you've had the worse strokes at my hand,
    You'll get the better cloth.'

Robin took off his gown of green,
  Which on Sir Guy he threw,
And he put on that horse's hide
  That clad him top to toe.

'Your bow, your arrows and little horn,
  All with me now I'll bear,
For now I'll go to Barnsdale,
  To see how my men may fare.'

Robin set Guy's horn to his mouth,
  And a loud blast he did blow,
That was heard by the Sheriff of Nottingham
  In the valley down below.

'Listen, listen,' said the sheriff,
  'I've heard no news but good,
For yonder I hear Sir Guy's horn blow,
  For he has killed Robin Hood.

'Yonder I hear Sir Guy's horn blow
  And it blows again this tide,
And yonder there comes that big yeoman,
  Dressed in his horse's hide.

'Come here, come here, my good Sir Guy,
  Ask what you will of me.'
'I want none of your gold,' says Robin Hood,
  'Nor none of your knights and fee,

'But now I have killed the master,' he said,
  'Let me go strike the knave.
That's all the reward that I will ask,
  And all that I would have.'

'You are a madman,' said the sheriff,
　'You could have had knights and fee,
But seeing your asking has been so poor,
　Well granted it shall be.'

Then Robin went up to Little John,
　He thought he'd set him loose,
But the sheriff and all his company
　Around him there drew close.

'Stand back! Stand back!' said Robin Hood.
　'Why do you draw so near?
It was never the custom of our country,
　A dead man's confession to hear.'

Robin pulled out an Irish knife,
　And loosed John hand and foot;
He gave him Sir Guy's bow in his hand,
　And bade him with it shoot.

Then John took an arrow in his hand
　And set it to his bow;
The sheriff saw Little John draw his bow,
　And he turned on his heel to go.

Towards his house in Nottingham
　He fled full fast away,
And so did all his company—
　Not one behind did stay.

But he could neither run so fast,
　Nor so fast away could go,
But Little John with an arrow broad
　Did cleave his heart in two.

Robin Hood's Death

As Robin Hood and Little John
    Went over a bank of broom,
Said Robin Hood to Little John,
    'We've shot for many a pound.

'But I cannot shoot but one shot more,
    My broad arrows will not fly;
But I have a cousin in merry Kirklees,
    Please God, she will bleed me.

'I'll neither eat nor drink,' said Robin,
    'Nor meat will do me no good,
Till I have been to merry Kirklees,
    My veins for to let blood.'

'I beg you not,' said Will Scarlock,
    'Dear master, do not do so,
Without half a hundred of your best bowmen
    Along with you to go.

'For there is a yeoman that lives in Kirklees
    That's sure to quarrel with you,
And if you have need of us, master,
    In faith, we will stand true.'

'If you're too scared now, William Scarlock,
    At home you'd better be.'
'If you are angry, my dear master,
    You'll never hear more of me.'

'Now there shall no man with me go,
  And no man with me ride,
But Little John shall be my man,
  And bear my bow by my side.'

'You can bear your bow yourself, master,
  And shoot for a penny with me.'
'I'll agree to that,' said Robin Hood,
  'And so, John, let it be.'

These two bold yeomen set off together,
  All day they went in rank,
Until they came to the Blackwater,
  And over it lay a plank.

Upon it there kneeled an old woman,
  That was cursing Robin Hood;
'Why do you curse Robin Hood?' said Robin,
  'Has he not done you good?'

'I have cause to curse,' said the old woman,
  'Though he has done me good,
For today he's going to fair Kirklees,
  His veins for to let blood.

'For Robin has been a lord of this land,
  And a friend to England's poor,
But the day he goes to fair Kirklees,
  He'll never be lord any more.'

'But we are going to merry Kirklees,
  There we may meet Robin Hood;
What message shall we take to him,
  That may yet do him good?'

'All this long day I've washed a shirt,
   It was made for Robin Hood,
And every wash I washed this shirt,
   The river has run with blood.

'All this long day I've washed this shirt
   For Robin that goes to be bled,
But before night falls at fair Kirklees,
   He'll be in his grave and dead.

'You may take this shirt,' said the old woman,
   'To give to Robin Hood;
We're weeping for his dear body,
   That this day must be let blood.'

'The prioress is my aunt's daughter,
   And is of my close kin;
I know she would do me no harm this day,
   For all the world to win.'

Then they went on, these yeomen two,
   And never once did cease,
But Robin was sick and sorrowful,
   When they came to fair Kirklees.

And when they came to fair Kirklees,
   They knocked upon the pin;
Up rose the lady prioress,
   To let good Robin in.

'Will you sit down, cousin Robin,' she said,
  'And drink some beer with me?'
'Nay, I'll neither eat nor drink,' he said,
  'Till I blood-letted be.'

Then Robin gave to the prioress
  Full twenty pound in gold,
And told her spend while that did last,
  And she should have more if she would.

'I have a room, cousin Robin,' she said,
  'Which you did never see,
And if you please to walk with me,
  Blood-letted you shall be.'

Down came the lady prioress,
  Her hands were white as milk;
The pair of blood-irons that she held,
  Were wrapped in the finest silk.

'Set a chafing dish to the fire,' she said,
  'And you roll up your sleeve.'
I think he is an unwise man
  That will no warning believe.

She laid the blood-irons to Robin Hood's vein,
  Alas, the more pity!
And pierced the vein, and let out the blood,
  That was so red to see.

And first it bled, the thick, thick blood,
   And afterwards the thin,
And well then knew good Robin Hood,
   That treason lay within.

He looked out from the window there,
   Where he might have got down,
But he was so weak he could not leap,
   And he could not get him down.

He looked upon his bugle-horn,
   Which hung down by his knee;
He put the horn up to his mouth,
   And blew out weak blasts three.

Then Little John said, when hearing him,
   As he sat under a tree,
'I fear my master is near dead,
   He blows so wearily.'

Then Little John went to fair Kirklees,
   Its doors he broke open wide,
And when he came to Robin Hood
   He knelt down by his side.

'What cheer, my master?' said Little John.
   'In faith, John, little good
I should never have come to fair Kirklees,
   This day for to let blood.

'For I gave my cousin gold so red,
  It was gold so red to see,
But not so red as my own heart's blood
  That she has bled from me.

'Today we shot for a penny,' said Robin,
  Under the greenwood tree,
But never again, dear Little John,
  Will you shoot for a penny with me.

'Go fetch me a priest,' said Robin Hood,
  'That will hear me confess,
For I may yet go to heaven on high,
  If the priest my life will bless.'

'I'd fetch for you a priest,' says John,
  'A priest who would bless you,
But they've barred the gates of fair Kirklees,
  And they will not let me through.'

Then Robin arose from where he lay,
  Though he was near to death,
Saying, 'I'll have a priest to bless my soul
  Before my dying breath.'

Then up jumped false Red Roger,
  Where he stood by the door,
'You'll never leave this room,' he said,
  'Till you lie dead on the floor.'

'I have a gown of green,' said Robin,
  'That by my knee hangs low,
And in my hand a flashing blade
  That can well bite at you.'

Robin Hood went to the window then
  And out of it would glide,
But Red Roger, with a sharpened spear,
  Thrust him through the milk-white side.

But Robin was nimble and light of foot,
  And thought to humble his pride,
For between his head and his broad shoulders
  He left a wound full wide.

Says, 'Lie there, lie there, Red Roger,
  Where the dogs they can you eat,
But I may get my blessing,' he said,
  'For I can still walk and speak.'

'But give me strength,' said Robin to John,
  'Give me your strength in my need,
And I trust to God in heaven so high
  Such a blessing will serve me indeed.'

'Now give me leave, give me leave,' said John,
  'For Christ's love, give leave to me,
To set a fire within this hall,
  And to burn up all Kirklee.'

'That I forbid,' said Robin Hood then,
  'Little John, it may not be;
I never hurt woman in all my life,
  Nor at my end shall it be.

'But give me my good bow in my hand,
  And a broad arrow I'll let flee,
And where this arrow is taken up,
  It's there my grave shall be.

'And take me up upon your back,
  And bear me along the street,
And dig for me a full fair grave
  Of gravel and of grit.

'And lay my bright sword at my head,
  My arrows at my feet,
And lay my yew bow by my side
  My yardstick with me to keep.

'Let me have length and breadth enough,
  With a green turf under my head,
That they may say, when I am dead
  Here lies bold Robin Hood.'

PLAYS OF ROBIN HOOD

Robin Hood and the Sheriff

(a fragment)

Enter the SHERIFF and SIR GUY.

SIR GUY:

>Sir Sheriff, I will take
>Robin Hood for your sake.

SHERIFF:

>I will give you gold and fee
>If you keep your word to me.

Exit the SHERIFF. Enter ROBIN HOOD.

SIR GUY:

>Robin Hood, fair and free,
>Let's shoot together under this tree.

ROBIN HOOD:

>To shoot with you I gladly will,
>All your wishes to fulfil.

SIR GUY shoots.

SIR GUY:

>See if you can hit.

ROBIN shoots.

ROBIN HOOD:

>My shot has it split.

SIR GUY:

Let's cast the stone

ROBIN HOOD:

So I will, by St John!

They cast stones (similar to shot put).

SIR GUY:

Let's cast the axle tree too.

They cast axle trees (similar to the caber toss).

SIR GUY:

Put your foot in front of you!

They wrestle. ROBIN throws SIR GUY to the ground.

ROBIN HOOD:

Ha! Sir knight, I've laid you flat.

SIR GUY:

And I shall pay you back for that.

They wrestle again, and SIR GUY throws ROBIN.

ROBIN HOOD:

Curse on you! I'll blow my horn.

SIR GUY:

You'll wish you never had been born.
Let's fight on to die or kill.

ROBIN HOOD:

He that flees, God send him ill!

They fight with swords, and ROBIN kills SIR GUY.

Now I've won and he is dead,
I'll cut off his wretched head.
This knight's clothes now I shall wear,
And in my hood his head I'll bear.

Exit ROBIN HOOD. Enter WILL SCARLOCK and LITTLE JOHN.

WILL SCARLOCK:
Well met, good friend, in the green wood!
What news is there of Robin Hood?

LITTLE JOHN:
Robin Hood and his company
By the sheriff were taken today.

WILL SCARLOCK:
We'll go after them with a will,
And the sheriff we will kill.

LITTLE JOHN and WILL SCARLOCK set off together.
Enter FRIAR TUCK and the SHERIFF with his MEN.

LITTLE JOHN:
Look there at Friar Tuck,
How well he can his bow pluck!

The SHERIFF's MEN take FRIAR TUCK,
and approach LITTLE JOHN and WILL SCARLOCK.

SHERIFF:
Yield now, for the sheriff's sake,
Or else your bows we shall break.

ROBIN HOOD AND THE SHERIFF

LITTLE JOHN and WILL SCARLOCK are caught and bound.

LITTLE JOHN:
>Now we are all bound the same.
>Good Friar Tuck, this is no game!

SHERIFF:
>You false outlaw, have no doubt,
>You shall be hanged and your guts pulled out.

WILL SCARLOCK:
>Now alas, what can we do?
>We must into the prison go.

The SHERIFF and his MEN escort the outlaws to Nottingham.

SHERIFF:
>Let the gates be opened wide,
>So we may bring these thieves inside.

*In the remainder of the play, ROBIN HOOD presumably rescues
LITTLE JOHN, WILL SCARLOCK and FRIAR TUCK from the gallows.*

The Play of Robin Hood

Here begins The Play of Robin Hood, very appropriate to be played in May Games.

ROBIN:

Now gather round my merry men all,
 And hear what I shall say:
Of an adventure I shall tell
 That happened the other day,
 As I went along the high way.

With a stout friar there I met,
 And a quarter-staff in his hand;
Lightly up to me he leapt,
 And ordered me to stand.

There were blows two or three
 And I can't tell who had the worse,
But I know for sure the bastard jumped me
 And he made off with my purse.

Is there any one of my merry men
 That to the friar will go,
And bring him to me here again,
 Whether he will or no?

LITTLE JOHN:

Aye, master! I make God a vow
 To that friar I'll go
And bring him here again to you,
 Whether he will or no.

THE PLAY OF ROBIN HOOD

Enter FRIAR TUCK hiccupping, with three dogs.

FRIAR TUCK:

Deus hic! Deus hic! God be here!
Is this not a holy word for a friar?
God save all this company!
But am I not a jolly friar?
For I can shoot both far and near,
And handle this sword and buckler here,
And this quarter-staff also.
If I meet with a gentleman or yeoman,
I'm not afraid to look him upon,
    Nor boldly with him to carp,
And if he should speak any words with me,
He shall get blows two or three,
    That shall make his body smart!

    But masters, to show you the reason
    Why I have come here this season,
    I'll tell you as I should:
I've come to seek a good yeoman,
In Barnsdale men say is his habitation.
    His name is Robin Hood,
And if that he be a better man than I,
His servant I'll be, and serve him truly,
But if that I be a better man than he,
Upon my soul, my knave he'll be,
    And lead these dogs all three!

ROBIN HOOD:

Yield now, friar, in your long coat!

ROBIN takes FRIAR TUCK in a neck hold.

FRIAR TUCK:

> Curse on you, knave, you're hurting my throat.

ROBIN HOOD:

> I think, friar, you're beginning to dote:
> Who made you so impudent and so bold
> To come into this forest here
>> Among my fallow deer?

FRIAR TUCK:

> Go pick your fleas, you ragged knave!
> If you make many words, I'll give you one upon the ear.
> Though I am only a poor friar,
> To seek Robin Hood I have come here,
>> And to break my heart to him.

ROBIN HOOD:

> You filthy friar, what do you want with him?
> He never loved a friar, nor none of friars' kin.

FRIAR TUCK:

> Be off, you ragged knave,
> Or I'll break your skin!

ROBIN HOOD:

> Of all the men to meet in the morning,
>> Friar, you're the worst!
> To meet with you I have no thirst,
> For he that meets a friar or a fox in the morning
>> May have bad luck that day,
>> So people say.
> Therefore I'd rather meet with the devil of hell—
>> Friar, I tell it as I think—
>> Than meet with a friar or a fox
>> In the morning, before I drink.

THE PLAY OF ROBIN HOOD

FRIAR TUCK:

Be off, you ragged knave, this is just said to mock!

If you make many words, you'll soon get a knock.

ROBIN HOOD:

Listen, friar, to what I say:

Over this water you must carry me,

Because the bridge has been swept away.

FRIAR TUCK:

I say nay, I will not;

To make you break your oath would be great pity and sin,

But a ride upon a friar's back you shall never win.

ROBIN HOOD:

Nay, get over!

ROBIN jumps on FRIAR TUCK's back.

FRIAR TUCK:

Now I am friar within, and you are Robin without,

To lay you here I have no great doubt.

FRIAR TUCK throws ROBIN in the water.

Now I am friar without, and you are Robin within,

Lie there knave, choose if you'll sink or swim.

ROBIN HOOD:

Why, you filthy friar! What did you do then?

FRIAR TUCK:

Indeed, I set a knave on his own feet again.

ROBIN HOOD:

You'll pay for that!

FRIAR TUCK:

Why! Do you want a fight?

ROBIN HOOD:

Aye, by God, that I might!

FRIAR TUCK:

Then have a go at Friar Tuck!

ROBIN and FRIAR TUCK fight.

ROBIN HOOD:

Hold your hand, friar, and hear me speak.

FRIAR TUCK:

Go on, ragged knave,
I think you're starting to sweat.

ROBIN HOOD:

In this forest I have a hound,
I wouldn't sell him for a hundred pound:
Give me leave my horn to blow
So that my hound may know.

FRIAR TUCK:

Blow on, ragged knave, without any doubt,
Blow till both your eyes pop out!

ROBIN blows on his horn; his MEN come in.

Here comes a bunch of ragged knaves,
All of them dressed in Kendal green,
And to you they take their way.

ROBIN HOOD:

Perhaps they do, as well they may.

FRIAR TUCK:

    I gave you leave to blow at your will,
    Now give me leave to whistle my fill.

ROBIN HOOD:

    Go whistle, friar, ill may you fare,
    Whistle until your eyes both stare.

FRIAR TUCK whistles and his men come in.

FRIAR TUCK:

    Now, Cut and Boss, bring out the clubs and staves,
    And down with those ragged knaves!

They ALL fight, and FRIAR TUCK'S MEN are beaten.

ROBIN HOOD:

    What do you say, friar, will you be my man,
    To do me the best service you can?
    You shall have both gold and fee,
    And here there is a lady too—

Enter MAID MARIAN.

    I will give her now to you,
    And her chaplain I do you make
    To service her all for my sake.

FRIAR TUCK:

    Here is a huckle-duckle
    An inch above the buckle.
    She is a trollop of trust
    To serve a friar at his lust,
    A pricker, a prancer, a tearer of sheets,
    A wagger of bollocks while other men sleeps.

Go home, you knaves, and set apples on the fire
For my lady and I will dance in the mire
For very pure joy!

FRIAR TUCK and MAID MARIAN dance, joined by the MEN of both sides.

SONG: *ROBIN HOOD'S DANCE*
Robin Hood, Robin Hood and Little John,
They leaned against a tree, ah!
Friar Tuck and Maid Marian
So turn about all three, ah!

'Robin Hood, Robin Hood,' said Little John,
'Come dance before the Queen, ah!
In a red petticoat and a green jacket,
A white hose and a green, ah!'

ROBIN HOOD:
Listen to me, my merry men all
And hear what I shall say
Of an adventure I shall you tell
That happened the other day.

With a proud potter I met
And a rose garland was on his head,
The flowers of it shone marvellous fresh.
For seven years and more he has used this way,
Yet was he never so courteous a potter
As one penny of passage to pay.

Is there any one of my merry men all
That would dare to be so bold
To make this potter pay for his passage,
Either in silver or gold.

LITTLE JOHN:
>Not I, master, for twenty pound ready told,
>For there is not one that I do know
>Dare mix it with that potter man-to-man.
>I felt his hand not long ago,
>But I had sooner been here with you,
>>Therefore I know what he is;
>Meet him when you will, or meet him when you may,
>He is as true a man as you'll mix with any day.

ROBIN HOOD:
>I'll wager with you, Little John, and twenty pound I'll bet
>That, when I have that potter met,
>I'll make him to pay passage yet.

LITTLE JOHN:
>You're on, Robin, I'll take your bet;
>If you can any passage get,
>Twenty pound I'll give you for your debt.

THE POTTER'S BOY JACK:
>Oh alas, that ever I saw this day!
>For I am far out of my way
>>From Nottingham Fair.
>>If I can't go any faster,
>The market will be done before I'm there.

ROBIN HOOD:
>Let me see. Are your pots whole and sound?

>>>*ROBIN throws the pots on the ground.*

JACK:
>Aye, master, but they will not break the ground!

ROBIN HOOD:

> I will them break
> For that cuckold your master's sake,
> And if they will break the ground
> I'll give you three pence for a pound.

JACK:

> Oh alas! What have you done?
> If my master comes, he'll break your crown.

THE POTTER:

> Why, you rascal! Are you still here?
> You should have been at Nottingham Fair.

JACK:

> I met with Robin Hood, a good yeoman;
> He has broken my pots
> And called you 'cuckold' for your name.

THE POTTER *to Robin Hood*:

> You may be a gentleman, so God me save,
> But to me you seem a worthless knave.
> You call me 'cuckold' for my name,
> But I swear by God and by my life,
> I've never even had a wife!

ROBIN HOOD:

> Listen, potter, what I shall say:
> For seven years and more you've used this way,
> Yet you were never so courteous to me
> As one penny of passage to pay.

THE POTTER:

> Why should you get a penny from me?

ROBIN HOOD:
>Because I am Robin Hood, chief governor
>>Under the greenwood tree.

THE POTTER:
>For seven years I've used this way up and down,
>Yet I paid passage to no man,
>Nor now will I begin, so do the worst you can.

ROBIN HOOD:
>Passage you must pay, here under the greenwood tree,
>Or else you must leave a pledge with me.

THE POTTER:
>If you're a good fellow, as men do you call,
>>Put away your bow,
>And take your sword and buckler in your hand,
>>And see what shall befall.

>*They fight, and THE POTTER has the better of it.*

ROBIN HOOD:
>Little John, where are you, now?

LITTLE JOHN:
>Here, master, I make God a vow.
>I told you, master, so God me save,
>That you would find the potter a knave.

THE POTTER:
>>That I can't deny!
>But if you're a good fellow, as men do you call,
>Take your sword and buckler in your hand,
>>And see what shall befall.

LITTLE JOHN *to Robin Hood*:

> Hold your buckler fast in your hand,
> And I will stiffly by you stand
>> Ready for the fight.
> Although the knave be never so stout,
> I shall rap him on the snout
>> And put him to flight.

They fight again, and now LITTLE JOHN and ROBIN have the better of it.

ROBIN HOOD:

> What do you say, potter, will you be my man,
> To do me the best service you can?

THE POTTER:

> I'll sell my horse, my harness, pots and panniers too;
> You'll have the one half, and I'll have the other.
> But if that's not enough for you,
> You'll get more blows, though you were my own brother.

ROBIN HOOD:

> Hold your hand! You shall have gold and fee,
> And join with us under the greenwood tree.

ALL exit together.

Thus ends the play of Robin Hood.

APPENDICES

A: Three fifteenth-century Chronicles

1. *Andrew of Wyntoun, An Original Chronicle of Scotland, Book VII, Chapter X (c.1408-20):*

> Little John and Robin Hood
> Were outlaws that were praised as good;
> In Inglewood and Barnsdale
> They used to travel the forest trail.

These lines form the last part of the entry for the year 1283, immediately before the entry for 1285. The preceding lines are about the earldom of Fife, and the following lines about the earldom of Mentieth—there is no obvious link between Robin Hood and either of these subjects.

The word 'wayth-men' translated here as 'outlaws' does not necessarily suggest a formal sentence of outlawry, and can even mean simply 'hunters'.

A more literal word-for-word translation of the final line would be, 'They used throughout this time to take their way.' Knight and Ohlgren suggest a translation along the lines of 'they practiced their labour' but, whilst this correctly translates possible meanings for the individual words, it misses the sense of the phrase; for a close parallel to the phrase 'oysyd ... thare trawale', see Barbour's Brus, X l.565/570. The phrase 'all this tyme' suggests that Robin Hood and Little John had lived in the forests before 1283, and may have continued to do so afterwards.

Nowhere else are these outlaws associated with Inglewood, which may be a mistake for Sherwood—Inglewood in Cumberland is considerably closer to the Scottish border so may have been a more familiar English forest name in Scotland, but has its own outlaw legend. There is no reason to believe the Barnsdale referred to here is anywhere other than Barnsdale in Yorkshire; Barnsdale in Rutland, which belonged to the Honour of Huntingdon, is known only as 'Bernard's Hill' until the mid-sixteenth century.

2. *Walter Bower,* Scotichronicon *(c.1440-47)*

from Chapter XX

Furthermore, everyone who was still fighting for Simon [de Montfort] was disinherited and outlawed, so the next year [1266], in less than one week the King of England transferred lands worth 17,560 nobles to others. The greater part of them took to the roads and highways, and turned to robbery. Then deadly warfare broke out between the king and the disinherited, such that manor houses were burned, towns destroyed, the countryside depopulated, churches ransacked, monks driven from the cloister, clerics blackmailed, the people ruined— no peace anywhere, no refuge anywhere, but desolation, misfortune, famine and plunder flourished.

At this time, that most celebrated assassin Robert Hood rose up and raised his head with Little John and his comrades among the disinherited and the banished. The foolish populace eagerly and wistfully make much of him in comedies and tragedies, and love to hear jesters and minstrels sing of him more than all other stories. Indeed praiseworthy deeds are told, as is seen in that once when he was in Barnsdale evading the king's anger and the prince's fury, he was hearing mass as was usual, and on no account wanted the service interrupted:

As he was hearing mass one day, a certain sheriff and officers of the king who had often attacked him before, tracked him to that remotest place in the forest. Some of his men who had noticed this came to him and urged him to make every effort to flee which, out of reverence for the sacrament that he was then devoutly venerating, he utterly refused to do, but the rest were trembling in terror of death. Robert was fearless, fully trusting in Him that he was worshipping, and with the few who then happened to be there, he took on his enemies and easily overcame them. And loaded with booty and ransoms, he always held priests and masses in higher regard thereafter, taking note of the saying, 'God heeds the one who often hears mass.'

from Chapter XXI

In the same year [1266] the disinherited English barons and the king's men were roving fiercely. Among them Roger de Mortimer took control in the Welsh Marches, and John de Eyville in the Isle of Ely. Robert Hood was now banished among the bushes and briars of the forest. Between them, they wrought great mayhem on monastic communities and the common people, the townspeople and the merchants.

If legends of Robin Hood had not remained popular until today, Walter Bower's testimony would probably be more widely accepted as straightforwardly factual. Bower seems familiar with a historical background to the legend that is not derived from ballad tradition. He is confident and categorical in his assertion that Robert Hood rose to prominence among the dispossessed after the Battle of Evesham. Bower also distinguishes Robert Hood from John de Eyville, who has sometimes been proposed as a 'real life' Robin Hood.

Bower treads a middle line between condemnation and adulation. He provides a tantalising summary of a lost ballad of Robin Hood from Scotland, which perhaps represents a yet earlier stage in the legend than surviving fifteenth-century ballads from England. As in 'Robin Hood and the Monk', Robin is so eager to hear Mass that it leads him into trouble, his ultimate success is attributed at least in part to his piety, and the strength of the merry men is shown to be dependent on his good leadership.

The phrase translated as 'that most celebrated assassin' has been translated elsewhere as 'the famous murderer' (A. I. Jones) 'that most famous murderer' (Watt et al.) and 'a well-known cut-throat' (Knight and Ohlgren).

3. Anonymous annotation to Ranulf Higden's Polychronicon (c.1461-70)

Around this time [c.1294-99] so the common people believe, a certain outlaw called Robin Hood and his comrades beleaguered Sherwood and other loyal areas of England with continual robberies.

This annotation appears at the bottom of a page covering events of the 1290s. Although the dating and context are somewhat vague compared with Bower's Scotichronicon, the annotator appears confident that in his day 'the common people' placed Robin Hood in the late thirteenth century. However, the annotator may have been reminded of Robin Hood by the events described on this page of the chronicle, including the destruction of forests used as hideouts by the Welsh and the uprising of William Wallace, which could be seen as parallel to the Robin Hood story. If so, the choice of page for the Robin Hood annotation may have less to do with simple chronology than might be supposed, and the opening words (circa hec tempore) apparently acknowledge that the date is only approximate.

Whereas both Wyntoun and Bower mention Barnsdale by name, this anonymous fifteenth-century annotation is the first chronicle entry to explicitly associate Robin with Sherwood ('shirwode'). Whilst early ballads more often place Robin Hood in Barnsdale, other early references to Sherwood appear in the ballad 'Robin Hood and the Monk' (c.1465) and in a verse of c.1400 in a manuscript from Lincoln Cathedral which predates the first mention of Barnsdale (see Appendix D).

B: A sixteenth-century Chronicle

John Mair (or Major), Historia Majoris Britanniæ
(published 1521)

Around this time as I suppose (*circa hæc tempora ut auguror*) Robert Hood the Englishman and Little John, notorious robbers, lurked in the woods seizing the belongings of only wealthy men; they didn't kill anyone except those who attacked them or fought back to protect their possessions. Through his plunder, Robert supported a hundred archers ready for action, and not four hundred of the strongest men would dare to attack them. The deeds done by this Robert are recounted in song by the whole of Britain. He would allow no woman to be molested, nor would he steal the belongings of the poor, indeed he provided for them sumptuously on rich pickings from the abbots. I condemn the man's robberies, but of all thieves he was the kindest and the prince.

This is no longer really chronicle at all. Even the supposed date in the reign of King Richard the Lionheart is admitted to be entirely conjectural. Rather than representing a historical tradition parallel to ballad tradition, Mair's account marks the start of the tradition of trying to place the legendary Robin Hood in an imagined historical context. All the details seem to be drawn from the songs which celebrate the hero's deeds, in which John Mair was apparently well versed. It also marks the moment when the legendary Robin Hood is said to have captured the imagination of 'the whole of Britain' rather than just the 'foolish populace'. There would still be stick-in-the-muds to disparage the songs of Robin Hood, but it is from this point that the legend begins to become respectable.

The new chronology for the outlaw which reimagines him in the reign of King Richard the Lionheart is part of this process, since it recasts the outlaw as a loyal supporter of the much-romanticised rightful king against a despised usurper. Although Robin's reconciliation with the young King Edward may have been part of the earlier legend, this is very different from the revised historical context in which he can oppose the illegitimate authority of John as regent, while still upholding royal authority in the exiled King Richard. With its anti-authoritarian message hidden, the legend becomes acceptable to all classes of society, including those it had previously criticised.

C: Some thirteenth-century legal records

Although not strictly-speaking sources for the legend, legal records can shed valuable light on its historical basis. The following selection draws on the work of David Pilling and Rob Lynley, whose permission is gratefully acknowledged. Many medieval legal documents include the name Robert Hood, but few can plausibly be linked with the outlaw of legend.

Pipe Roll 74, York, 1225

> The sheriff owes 32s. 8d. in respect of the chattels of Robert Hood, fugitive.

At some prior date, the possessions of Robert Hood had been seized because he was a fugitive from justice. There is no indication of what Robert's original crime may have been, and no further records indicate that he was ever brought to justice. There is nothing exceptional in this record, and Robert is named not because of any notorious crime but as a handy reference for a particular debt. Further records suggest the debt went unpaid until 1234. The next two entries in the Pipe Roll list two other fugitives whose goods have been seized, because money is also owed in respect of their property. One of these is a 'Willelmus Warin' who may possibly be William Fitz Warin, brother of Fulk Fitz Warin of Whittington.

Coincidentally, a Robert Hod is fined in the same year for damage to a sheepfold at Shenley, Buckinghamshire. It is highly unlikely that both cases refer to the same man, which illustrates the folly of basing arguments about a supposed 'real Robin Hood' in legal records rather than legendary sources. Not every Robert Hood is Robin Hood.

Chancery Inquisitions, 199, 1254

Writ to the Sheriff of York to inquire as to the persons who in the company of Richard de Riparia and others during the vacancy of the Abbey of Byland came to the grange of the said abbey at Fawdington and threw down a certain dyke on Pilmoor, rooted up a hedge, and carried off the bars of the door and part of the hay ...

Inquisition as to the throwing down of a dyke etc. at the at the grange of Fawdington on Pilmoor ... Robert Hod ... [and nearly 80 others] are the persons who committed the offences above mentioned, saving that the jury know nothing of the carrying away of bars or hay.

This appears to have been a local territorial dispute, which was settled next year when Richard de Riparia (or 'de la Ryver') granted the Abbot of Byland common pasture in 300 acres of the moorland of Pilmoor. If the Robert Hod in this document is indeed our Robin Hood, then his involvement here would seem to be purely random and incidental.

Legal documents relating to the robbery of Saero de Gargrave, c.1260–62

King's Bench Plea Roll 49/50, 1265-66

York: The same Saero [de Garvgrave] comes for four days against … Robert Hod [and nine or more others] … that they took the goods and chattels of the aforesaid Saero at Ottringham and Hedon …

King's Bench Plea Roll 52, 1268

York: Saerus de Gargrave comes for four days against … Robert Hod [and eight or more others] … for taking the plaintiff's goods and chattels at Hedon and Ottringham against the peace of the lord king, and that they took wine and cattle and other possessions belonging to Saerus contrary to the peace, and that all of the aforementioned offenders defaulted on a summons before the king's court on a certain day (in 1262) …

Robert John stood surety for Robert Hod … and that Robert Hod defaulted and his surety was fined [??] shillings …

Ottringham and Hedon are in Holderness (Yorkshire, East Riding) which, according to the Chronicle of Meaux, was the scene of disturbances against the king in about 1260, and at least one of Robert Hod's co-accused is known to have played a prominent part in this rebellion. Saero de Gargrave apparently opposed the rebels and suffered as a result.

Assize Roll 83, Cambridge, 1269

... that Peter Giffard was on the island, and was in service to
Roger son of Robert ...

... that Robert Hod was on the island with Roger son of Robert,
and inquiry is made as to their chattels, and William Page
likewise.

*This assize roll lists Robert Hod among the dispossessed who had fought for
Simon de Montfort and had taken refuge on the Isle of Ely. Robert is with
his son Roger, and Robert and Roger each appear to be accompanied by a
retainer.*

D: Some early allusions to the legend

Piers Plowman, 1377

> I don't know properly my Pater Noster as the priest may sing it,
> But I know rhymes of Robin Hood and Randolf, Earl of Chester.

These words are spoken by the character of Sloth. As with many other allusions to the outlaw legend, the point is that people are more interested in Robin Hood than in religion. The Pater Noster is the Latin text of the Lord's Prayer.

In Passione Domini, Hugo Legat, c.1399–1404

> For many men, I'm told, speak of Robin Hood that shot never in
> his bow.

The meaning is that people hold forth on subjects they do not fully understand. Legat is denouncing speakers who impress their audience with Classical allusions without knowing their true significance.

Geoffrey Chaucer apparently alluded to the same proverb in his poem Troilus and Criseyde *(c.1386):*

> ... people such as that, I guess,
> Disparage Love that nothing of him know;
> They speak, but they bent never his bow!

Lincoln Cathedral MS 132, c.1400

> Robin Hood in Sherwood stood,
> Hooded and hatted, stockinged and shod,
> Four and thirty arrows he bore in his hands.

These lines were written in both English and Latin by an untrained hand.

Dives and Pauper, c.1405–10

> For the people these days ... had rather go to the tavern than to
> holy church, rather to hear a song of Robin Hood or of some
> ribaldry than to hear Mass or Matins or anything of God's
> service or any word of God.

Dives and Pauper *is a commentary on the Ten Commandments written as a dialogue between a wealthy layman and a poor priest or friar.*

The Reply of Friar Daw Topias, c.1420
    In old English it is said,
      'Unkissed is unknown,'
    And, 'Many men speak of Robin Hood,
      And shot never in his bow.'
This poem responds to an early fifteenth century invective against friars,
written under the name Jack Upland. With these lines, Friar Daw dismisses
a question by suggesting that Jack doesn't know what he's talking about.

Legal Yearbook, c.1429
    Robin Hood in Barnsdale stood.
The earliest example of a phrase that recurs in legal texts for three centuries.

Wiltshire Parliamentary Return, 1432
    Adam Bell, Clym of the Clough, William of Cloudsley,
    Robin Hood in green wood stood, good man was he,
    Little John, Much, the miller's son, Scarlock, Reynoldine.
The first three names belong to a separate legend of the outlaws of Inglewood.

The Compound of Alchemy, George Ripley, 1471
    ... many men speak with wondering,
    Of Robin Hood, and of his bow,
    That never shot therein, I know.

A burlesque on Robin Hood balladry, c.1458–1500
    Robin Hood in Barnsdale stood,
    He leaned against a maple thistle
    Then came Our Lady and sweet St Andrew
    Are you asleep or awake, Geoffrey Cook?

    A hundred winters the water was broad,
      I cannot tell you how deep
    He took a goose neck in his hand
      And over the water he went.

[He jumped up to a thistle top
And cut himself a holly club;
He struck the wren between the horns,
So fire sprang out of the pig's tail]

Jack boy, is your bow broken,
Or has any man done you wretched wrong?
[He plucked mussels out of a willow,
   And put them into his satchel.

Wilkin was an archer good,
   And well could he handle a spade,]
He took his bent bow in his hand
   And sat down by the fire.

[He took with him three score bows and ten,
A piece of beef, another of bacon,
Of all the birds in merry England,
So merrily sings the merry bottle.]

My lady began to spin a thread,
Her nose was all askew to the south
Who dares to be so dare-devil
As to crack under the walls of Dover?

This ludicrous piece lampoons Robin Hood balladry and other late-medieval
popular song. It has long been known from Rastell's Interlude of the Four
Elements *(1519), where it is sung by the character of Ignorance.*
An unrelated manuscript source was identified by Holt and Takamiya, which
must have been written after 1457 and probably before c.1500. Passages in
square brackets appear only in Rastell's version; the last verse appears only
in the manuscript version.

Sermon for 20th Sunday after Trinity, c.1500

Many of these lay people despise priesthood, and they take no heed of the word of God. They give no credence to the scripture of Almighty God. They take more heed of these wanton prophets as Thomas of Erceldoune or Robin Hood and such simple matters, but they give not so much credence to the prophets of God, as Isaiah, Jeremy, David, Daniel, and to all the twelve prophets of God.

Thomas of Erceldoune reputedly spent seven years with the Queen of Elfland, and returned with the gift of prophecy. This Robin Hood allusion was recently identified by Henrik Nielsen of the International Robin Hood Bibliography.

A Hundred Merry Tales, c.1524/5

'So it is, that my spiritual father has made it my penance to fast every Friday on bread and water till I can say my Pater Noster. Therefore, I beg you, teach me my Pater Noster, and upon my word, I shall teach you in return a song of Robin Hood that shall be worth twenty of it!'

Just like the character of Sloth in Piers Plowman *150 years before, this young man cannot say his Pater Noster, but he does know rhymes of Robin Hood and values them more highly than prayer.*

The Image of Ipocrysy, Part III, c.1533

They finger their fiddles
And cry in quinibles [*musical fifths*]
'Away these Bibles,
For they be but riddles!
And give them Robin Hood,
To read how he stood
In merry green wood,
When he gathered good,
Before Noah's Flood!'

E: Music for ballads and songs

The traditional tunes associated with the Robin Hood ballads do not necessarily reflect the original tunes. Since all the ballads are written in a form of 'ballad metre' it is easy enough to marry old words to a new tune, or *vice versa*, and many early printed ballads advertise that they have been set to a new tune. Medieval 'ballads' (a modern term) may not have been sung, and 'Robin Hood and the Monk' describes itself as a 'talking' rather than a song (v.93).

The music for 'Robin Hood and Allen a Dale' is the first half of the popular seventeenth-century tune, 'Drive the cold winter away'. Rimbault is elusive on the subject of the tune's connection with the ballad, and it may be a case of wishful thinking.

Robin Hood's Birth
The Birth of Robin Hood

adapted from Christie, 1876

There's ma - ny that speak of grass, of grass, And ma - ny that speak of

corn, And ma - ny that sing of Ro - bin Hood, But know lit - tle where he was

born. His fa-ther was an earl's stew-ard, That served for meat and fee; His

mo - ther was Earl Hun-ting-don's daugh-ter, A la - dy fair and free.

Robin Hood and the Foresters
Robin Hood's Progress to Nottingham

adapted from tradition

Earl Ran - dolf kept Ro - bin for fif - teen win - ters,

Der - ry, der - ry down, Un - til he was fif - teen years old, And

Ro - bin grew in - to a big fel - low, Of

cou - rage sto - ut and - bold. Hey down, der - ry, der - ry down.

Robin Hood and the Curtal Friar
In Summer Time

perhaps c.1611-50

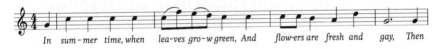

In sum - mer time, when lea - ves gro - w green, And flow-ers are fresh and gay, Then

Ro - bin Hood and his mer - ry men They went to sport and play.

Robin Hood and the Pinder

from the Gostling lute manuscript, c.1600-50

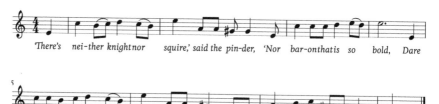

'There's nei-ther knight nor squire,' said the pin-der, 'Nor bar-on that is so bold, Dare take a ram-ble to the town of Wake-field, But he pays a pledge to the pin - fold.'

Robin Hood and Allen a Dale

adapted from Rimbault's transcription

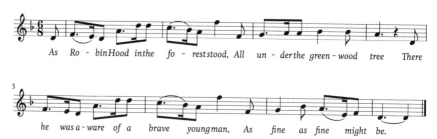

As Ro - bin Hood in the fo - rest stood, All un - der the green - wood tree There he was a-ware of a brave young man, As fine as fine might be.

Robin Hood and the Bishop of Hereford

from a broadside of Daniel Wright, Holborn, c.1709-34

Oh, some they will talk of lords and-knights And some of ba - rons - bold, But I'll tell you how Ro-bin Hood served the bi-shop, When he robbed him of his gold.

Robin Hood and the three Squires

traditional (Staffordshire, 1845)

There are twelve months in all the year, As I hear peo - ple say, But the

mer - ri - est month in all the year Is the mer - ry month of May.

Robin Hood's Death

traditional (Virginia, 1929)

As Ro - bin Hood and Lit - tle John Went o - ver a bank of broom, Said

Ro - bin Hood to Lit - tle John, 'We've shot for ma - ny a pound. 'But

I can - not shoot but one shot mo-re, My broad ar - rows will not fly; But

I have a cou - sin in mer - ry Kirk - le - es, Please God, she will bleed me.

257

Robin Hood, I

adapted from Giles Lodge's Lute Book, c.1575

Ro - bin Hood, Ro - bin Hood, and Lit-tle John, They leaned a - gainst a tree, ah!

Fri - ar Tuck and Maid Ma-ri-an, So turn a - bout all three, ah!

Robin Hood, II

adapted from Cobbold's 'New Fashions', c.1581-1639

Ro - bin Hood, Ro - bin Hood and Lit-tle John, They lean-ed a-gainst a tree, ah!

Fri - ar Tuck and Maid Ma - ri - an So turn a - bout, all three, ah!

Robin Hood, III

from Ravenscroft's 'A Round of three Country Dances', 1609

Ro - bin Hood, Ro - bin Hood said Lit-tle John, Come dance be-fore the queen, ah!

In a red pet - ti-coat and a green jac - ket, A white hose and - a green, ah!

These three versions of the tune 'Robin Hood' are all from the late sixteenth or early seventeenth century, but show enough divergence to suggest the tune had been known for some time before it was first recorded. The second two versions are broadly similar but, whilst the first belongs to the same family, it represents a very different branch of the tree.

The music in Giles Lodge's Lute Book is written for the lute with elaborate ornamentation intended for a sophisticated audience. It has been recast here as a popular dance tune in a regular AABB form. Words have been added from Cobbold. In Cobbold's original text, instead of a final syllable 'ah', the last two words of each line are repeated ('a tree, a tree') but each line is sung only once.

Bibliography

Alexander, James W. 1982, 'Ranulf III of Chester: An Outlaw of Legend?' in *Neuphilologische Mitteilungen* Vol. 83 No. 2

Basdeo, Stephen, 2019, *Robin Hood: The Life and Legend of an Outlaw*

Bond, Edward A. (ed.) 1867, *Chronica Monasterii de Melsa*, Vol. II

Burgess, Glyn S. 2005, 'I kan rymes of Robyn Hood, and Randolf Erl of Chestre' in *"De sens rassis": Essays in Honor of Rupert T. Pickens*

Chappell, W. 1840, *A Collection of National English Airs*

Child, Francis James (ed.) 1882-98, *English and Scottish Popular Ballads*, Vol. III

Christie, W. 1876, *Traditional Ballad Airs*, Vol. I

Davis, A. K. 1929, *Traditional Ballads of Virginia*

Dobson, R. B. and J. Taylor, 1976, *Rymes of Robin Hood*

Giles, Rev. J. A. (ed.) 1854, *Matthew Paris's English History, from the year 1235 to 1273*, Vol. III

Gutch, John Matthew (ed.) 1850, *The Robin Hood Garlands and Ballads*, Vol. II

Hahn, Thomas G. (ed.) 2000, *Robin Hood in Popular Culture: Violence, Transgression, and Justice*

Holt, J. C. 1982, 1989, *Robin Hood*

Holt, J. C. and T. Takamiya, 1989, 'A New Version of A Rhyme of Robin Hood' in *English Manuscript Studies 1100-1700*, Vol. I

Jacob, E. F. 1925, 'Presentments by the Jury of Cambridge before William de St. Omer and his colleagues, 1269' in *Studies in the Period of Baronial Reform and Rebellion, Oxford Studies in Social and Legal History*, Vol. VIII (ed. Sir Paul Vinogradoff)

Knight, Stephen, 1994, *Robin Hood: A Complete Study of the English Outlaw*

Knight, Stephen, 1998, *Robin Hood: The Forresters Manuscript*

Knight, Stephen and Thomas H. Ohlgren, 1997, *Robin Hood and Other Outlaw Tales*

Laing, David (ed.) 1872, *The Orygynale Chronykil of Scotland by Androw of Wyntoun*, Vol. II

Leigh, James Wentworth, 1901, 'Hereford Cathedral: second paper' in *Good Words*, Vol. 42, London (Dec 1901): 844-850.

Luxford, Julian M. 2009, 'An English chronicle entry on Robin Hood' in *Journal of Medieval History* 35 (2009) 70-76

Midgley, Tim, 2018 (2006) 'An Alternative location for 'Saylis' of the Geste' online: http://midgleywebpages.com/saylis.html

Morrison, Stephen (ed.) 2012, *A Late Fifteenth-Century Sermon Cycle*

Nielsen, Henrik Thiil, 2019, "Coresed' and 'Frese': Two cruces in *A Gest of Robin Hood*' in *Notes and Queries*, Vol. 66, Issue 3

Ohlgren, Thomas H. 2007, *Robin Hood: The Early Poems, 1465-1560: Texts, Contexts, and Ideology*

Pilling, David, 2020, *Rebellion Against Henry III: The Disinherited Montfortians, 1265-1274*

Public Record Office, 1916, *Calendar of Inquisitions Miscellaneous (Chancery)*

Public Record Office, 1957, *Curia Regis Rolls of the Reign of Henry III*

Rimbault, Edward Francis, 1850, 'Musical Illustrations of the Robin Hood Ballads' in Gutch 1850

Robinson, Chalfant (ed.) 1927, *The Great Roll of the Pipe for the fourteenth Year of the Reign of King Henry III*

Sussex, Lucy, 1994, 'References to Robin Hood up to 1600' in Knight, 1994

Walz, Robert B. 2013, *The Gest of Robyn Hode: A Critical and Textual Commentary*

Online resources:

Allen W. Wright, *Robin Hood, Bold Outlaw of Barnsdale and Sherwood*
boldoutlaw.com

Henrik Thiil Nielsen, *International Robin Hood Bibliography*
irhb.org

Robert Fortunaso, *Robin Hood, the Facts and the Fiction*
robinhoodlegend.com

Stephen Basdeo, *Here Begynneth A Lytell Geste of Robin Hood*
gesteofrobinhood.com

Glossary

amble: *an ambling gait in a horse is faster than a walk, but much smoother than a trot.*

axle tree: *the timber axle of a cart or wagon.*

blood-letting: *drawing off blood as a medical treatment based on the theories of Galen.*

blood-irons: *a tool for blood-letting.*

buckler: *a small round shield.*

chafing dish: *a small pan set over a burner.*

coffer: *a small chest for storing money and valuables.*

courser: *a strong, fast horse suitable for a knight.*

courtesy: *the medieval system of courtly ideals, manners and behaviours.*

forester: *a forest official, a gamekeeper.*

friar: *a member of a religious brotherhood devoted to working in the community; used in its literal sense 'brother' for a monk or abbot.*

knave: *a servant, a commoner, a rogue.*

lancegay: *a light spear or lance.*

ling: *a variety of heather.*

livery: *the official dress or uniform given by a lord to his retainers; the action of giving livery.*

mantle: *a cloak.*

mark: *an amount of money equivalent to 160 pence (160d.) or two thirds of a pound; the target or spot aimed at by an archer.*

Michaelmas: *the feast of St Michael the Archangel on 29th September.*

nock: *the notched end of an arrow which is fitted to the bowstring.*

outlaw: *a person stripped of all legal rights and protections.*

palfrey: *a light, graceful riding horse, often with an ambling gait.*

pinder: *the keeper of a pinfold, responsible for impounding stray livestock.*

pinfold: *a secure enclosure, pound or pen for stray livestock.*

pledge: *a surety, an item left in pawn, a promise.*

pluck buffet: *a game played by the outlaws, with buffets or blows as forfeits.*

scarlet: *a fine woollen cloth, usually but perhaps not always dyed with red kermes.*

score: *twenty; thus, seven score is 140.*

shilling: *an amount of money equivalent to 12 pence (12d.); there are twenty shillings in a pound.*

shoot about: *to shoot arrows from one target to another and back again.*

tine: *the point of an antler; older, stronger stags have more tines.*

trestle tree: *a tree fitted with a crossbeam in its branches as a hidden seat for a hunter.*

yeomanry: *the class of free smallholders or peasants and artisans; an implicit code of conduct associated with the yeoman class.*

yeoman of the crown: *a member of the king's household.*

Ingram Content Group UK Ltd.
Milton Keynes UK
UKHW041633200323
418860UK00002B/180